The Book *of*
HORRIBLE
Questions

Also by SMITH AND DOE

What Men Don't Want Women to Know

The Book *of* HORRIBLE *Questions*

Everyone Has a Price— What's Yours?

SMITH AND DOE

St. Martin's Griffin
New York

Library of Congress Cataloging-in-Publication Data

Smith.
    The book of horrible questions : everyone has a price,
  what's yours / Smith and Doe.
        p.   cm.
    ISBN: 0-312-20434-5
    1. Self-interest—Moral and ethical aspects Humor.
  2. Questions and answers Humor. 3. Selfishness Humor.
  4. Ethics Humor.
  I. Doe, Bill. II. Title.
  PN6231.S493S64   1999
  081—dc21   99-20473
                                                      CIP

First St. Martin's Griffin Edition: June 1999

10   9   8   7   6   5   4   3   2   1

This book is
dedicated to the
813
horrible human
beings who
answered these
questions.

First,
A Word,

SMITH AND DOE are painfully aware that some people will see this book as yet another reminder of our lack of morals, values, and good taste.

After weathering a massive backlash from our last book, we attempted suicide. *Fortunately, attending strip clubs for three consecutive sleepless days was not fatal.* Now after a year of intensive therapy, we are again ready to act as human shields, bearing the brunt of the tidal wave of revulsion that will devastate our lives when you, the average man and woman, are confronted with yet another face of the darkness that lurks within you.

The key to your success in using this book is the degree of *total honesty* with which you answer the questions. Take each question seriously. Imagine the amounts of money you will make or give up as *really belonging* to you. Imagine the often painful discomforts described herein as *actually happening* to you (or, in many cases, to the poor sap that you sacrifice for your own personal gain). Weigh carefully the benefits or consequences of each choice you make.

The scope of these questions is designed to chart the substantive, measurable levels to which you will actually sink in pursuit of money, self-promotion, or avoidance of personal pain and discomfort. By looking into your own heart through

x

the metaphor of these questions you will ultimately be able to determine how greedy, morally bankrupt, untrustworthy, and selfish you truly are.

And now, **SMITH AND DOE** urge you to raise your pant legs as you begin your trek through the murky swamp that is the human psyche and, at times, close your eyes . . . because what you're about to see ain't pretty.

Karmic Guarantee

SMITH AND DOE provide a money-back guarantee that by answering the following questions honestly **there will be NO karmic repercussions** (meaning that nothing bad will happen to you because you theoretically elected to do vicious harm unto others, including but not limited to family members, best friends, lovers, and/or pets). All dollar amounts denoted below are tax free, and will be deposited into your account without a trace.

THESE QUESTIONS ARE NOT FOR THE FAINT OF HEART. They are despicable questions, forcing each of us to ask ourselves just how far we would go for the almighty dollar, and what standards of ethics and morals we would sacrifice for personal gain.

SMITH AND DOE dare ask you to answer HONESTLY, and face the horrible truth of the evil that lurks within each of us.

The most important thing to keep in mind about all the hideous things you may say you would do is:

NO ONE WILL
EVER KNOW

Note from the Management

These questions were given to over 800 people in all walks of life who responded anonymously, and the results are included. Their views do not necessarily represent the views of SMITH AND DOE (especially the part about eating a foot).

THANK YOU

Chapter One

Big Ticket Items

The amounts in this category are so astronomically gener-
ous you will be tempted to take the money and run, conse-
quences be damned. Don't give in too easily. Carefully
evaluate what the money will do for you as opposed to the
sacrifice you will make.

We begin with . . .

1. **$10,000,000:** If you accept this money, you will die of natural causes on your birthday at age 70. You won't live a day longer than that and you will die in your sleep, peacefully, guaranteed.

2. **$5,000,000:** Same as above, except you'll live to be 75.

3. **$1,000,000:** Same as above, except you'll live to be 80.

4. **$100,000,000:** You will die at age 100, but it will be a hideously painful, long (two straight days) and tortuous death.

5. **$7,500,000:** Your mate will be kidnapped and held like the kid in *Ransom* (a filthy bed and only the most basic of foods) FOR ONE YEAR. There is a guarantee of no physical harm as well as no sexual contact. When the year is up, YOU will rescue the mate that you profitably condemned and reap all the loving benefits of doing so. No one will ever know you had anything to do with it, and you just made $7.5 mil, *although you risk the chance that he/she* **may** *suffer some degree of recurring trauma (i.e., waking up in the middle of the night in a cold sweat, screaming).*

6. **$100,000:** A funeral is taking place. You do not know anyone at the funeral or anyone involved with it. As a family member is making their heartfelt, teary speech, you must run into the midst of the crowd and yell, "I'M GLAD HE'S DEAD! HA HA HA HA!!!" and then run away.

Smith
and
Doe

How You Stack Up

1. To get the $10,000,000,
   7% would kick the bucket at age 70.

2. To get the $5,000,000,
   8% would buy the farm at 75.

3. To get the $1,000,000,
   54% would take a dirt nap at 80.

4. For $100,000,000,
   46% would be tortured to death at 100.

5. For $7,500,000,
   38% would have their mate kidnapped and then
   fake the rescue.

6. For $100,000,
   85% would disrupt a funeral, causing massive emo-
   tional damage.

7. **$1,500,000:** Dig up the grave site and get caught by the police. You may never tell anyone you did it for money and must come up with some other excuse.

8. **$1,000,000:** Dig up the grave site and suck the marrow out of one of the dead person's bones. (Either Smith, Doe, or their duly appointed representative must witness the sucking and confirm that the bone is empty—only then will the money be wired into your account.)

☺ ☺ ☺

9. MEN $1,000,000; WOMEN $500,000: You must attend a hard-core prison for one month with no special protection or provisions. There will be nothing on your criminal record when you are released.

10. MEN $1,500,000; WOMEN $1,000,000: Same as above, except you will share a cell with Long Dong Silver.

11. MEN AND WOMEN $2,000,000: Same as above, except you must do something to piss off the Aryan Brotherhood (for men) or Hell's Angels' Sisters (for women).

12. $10,000,000: Same as above, except you will share a cell with a man who was jailed for brutally raping 42 men who look exactly like you.

☺ ☺ ☺

13. **$250,000:** Wearing your seat belt and driving any normal sedan equipped with air bags, you must drive your car at 40 miles per hour into a lamppost.

14. **$350,000:** Same as above, except 50 miles per hour.

15. **$5,000,000:** Same as above, except you must do it at 50 miles per hour with a small leak in the gas tank.

4 How You Stack Up

7. 54% would become a grave digger and get caught by the police.

8. 8% would suck marrow out of the dead body's bones.

9. 23% would spend a full month in a hard-core prison.

10. 24% would share a cell with a known homosexual . . .

11. 15% . . . and piss off the Aryan Brotherhood.

12. 9% would share the cell with a homosexual AIDS carrier.

13. 55% would drive a car into a lamppost at 40 miles per hour.

14. 46% would do it at 50 miles per hour.

15. 31% would do it at 50 miles per hour with a small leak in the gas tank.

16. $250,000: Think of the most physically repugnant person you know. Say their name aloud. Now, to get paid, you must let that person squat above you and release a large helping of diarrhea onto your chest. You must then wait for five minutes, breathing only through your nose. Then you may get up, get showered, and get paid.

17. $500,000: Same as above, except a good portion of the diarrhea will splatter onto your face.

18. $750,000: Same as above, except the person has just returned from an all-you-can-eat corn-and-nut-eating contest.

☺ ☺ ☺

19. $5,000,000 (WOMEN ONLY): You will never be able to have a child, but you may adopt.

20. $10,000,000 (WOMEN ONLY): You must give your firstborn child up for adoption. (Double the amount if you keep it for a year first.)

21. $5,000,000 (MEN ONLY): You will never be able to have a child, but you may adopt.

22. $50,000 (MEN ONLY): You must give your firstborn child up for adoption.

☺ ☺ ☺

23. $5,000,000: You must be the target in a knife-throwing act in a circus, only the man who will throw five razor-sharp knives at your head from ten paces away has only practiced on stuffed dummies (but with great success).

24. $7,500,000: You must be the clown chased by Brahman bulls in the rodeo, only there are no other clowns to distract the enraged bulls nor anything of any kind to hide in. When you have successfully outrun 5 bulls for 3 minutes each, collect your SMITH AND DOE prize money.

6 How You Stack Up

16. 77% chose diarrhea on their chest.

17. 38% would let it splatter on their face . . .

18. 38% . . . after the shitter returns from a corn-and-nut-eating contest.

19. 50% of the women would never be able to have a child.

20. 0% of the women would give up their firstborn for adoption.

21. 45% of the men would never have a child.

22. 9% of the men would give their firstborn up for adoption. (For a small fee SMITH AND DOE will release the names of these 9% of men to the general public.)

23. 15% would let the knife thrower test his skills with their head in the target area.

24. 22% would get chased by the bulls.

25. $10,000,000: Allow yourself to be bound in a strait-jacket, shackled and lowered upside down into Houdini's Chinese water torture tank. You have 3 minutes to escape and claim $10 million.

26. $10,000,000: Have one foot amputated and surgically attached to your butt-cheek, then shave your body entirely bald and tour with Dr. Arnold Ehret's Traveling Freak Show as the Hairless Butt-Footed Boy (or Girl) for 2 full years, during which time you can never tell anyone you were not born that way. When you have completed your tour, the cash is yours (and you are free to do all the corrective plastic surgery you wish).

☺ ☺ ☺

27. $500,000: A human pancreas will be put on a plate in front of you. You must eat it. When it's gone, you get paid.

28. $750,000: Same as above, except it's a two-foot section of a large intestine. (Double the offer if it's uncleaned.)

29. $1,000,000: Same as above, except it's a human foot. (The bone has been removed.)

☺ ☺ ☺

30. $100,000: Perform natural sexual acts with a reasonably attractive partner at a live sex club with your family and friends in attendance.

31. $500,000: Same as above, except you must perform *unnatural* sex acts.

32. $750,000: Same as above, except you must perform natural sex acts with a 90-year-old man or woman.

33. $1,000,000: Same as above, except you must perform *unnatural* sex acts with the 90 year old.

How You Stack Up

25. 11% would brave the Chinese water torture.

26. 42% would attach their foot to their butt-cheek and join the circus.

27. 69% would chow a pancreas.

28. 38% elected to munch intestines.

29. 33% would dine on deboned foot.

30. 37% would do a live sex act . . .

31. 11% . . . would include *unnatural* acts.

32. 10% would perform a sex act with a 90 year old.

33. 12% would include *unnatural* sex acts with the 90 year old.

(SMITH AND DOE wish to note the bizarre phenomenon of a preference for *unnatural* sex acts with a 90-year-old partner.)

Chapter Two

Torture

(You have one choice and one choice only.)

This category isn't about money. You don't have the luxury of turning your nose up and saying, "No, thanks." The choices that confront you here will truly begin to warm you to the reality of just how hideously evil you really are . . .

1. This will give you an idea of your value as a brother:
   A. Your sister gets carjacked and gang-raped but survives;
   or,
   B. Your left testicle gets slowly crushed in a vise. Which do you choose?
2. For sisters:
   A. Your brother gets committed to a mental asylum for life;
   or,
   B. With no anesthetic, your left breast is sawed off by the neighborhood butcher.
3. *How* much did you say you love your parents?
   A. *You* lose everything you own and are reduced to a beggar;
   or,
   B. Your parents endure 30 seconds of an electric cattle prod up their butts.
4. How much do you lust for success?
   A. You win a new Rolls-Royce convertible, but must beat your head against a brick wall until unconscious to get it;
   or,
   B. You win a used Hyundai and dinner at Pup 'n' Taco.
5. How far will soul mates go?
   A. Your mate contracts a painful, untreatable, though invisible skin disease;
   or,
   B. Your dentist extracts 4 of your teeth (of your own choosing) using carpenter's tools with no anesthetic.

How You Stack Up

1. Send your sister to be gang-raped with your blessing: 53%

   ... *or* have your left testicle crushed in a vice: 47%.

2. Commit your brother to a mental asylum: 78%

   ... *or* have your left breast sawed off by Bob, the neighborhood butcher: 22%.

(SMITH AND DOE wish to note the ease with which women commit their brothers to mental asylums and urge men to take this into account when considering the gang-rape option.)

3. Lose everything and start begging: 50%

   ... *or* send the cattle prod up your parent's butts: 50%.

4. Beat your head until you are unconscious to win a Rolls-Royce: 26%

   ... *or* dine at Pup 'n' Taco instead: 74%.

5. Cause your mate to contract a disease: 48%

   ... *or* have four teeth pulled with no anesthetic: 52%.

6. How much do you really care about humanity?

A. An earthquake makes California break off and fall into the sea, killing millions of innocent people;

or,

B. A careless nurse sticks a red-hot needle deep into your eye.

7. Let's see what kind of friend you really are:

A. Your best friend is framed and sentenced to death for a murder he or she did not commit;

or,

B. Your left foot is submerged in boiling water for five full, excruciatingly painful minutes (an experience that will undoubtedly cause irreparable nerve damage).

8. How much do you revere Mother Nature?

A. A helpless seal is bashed over the head then hung up and skinned alive, while its three newborn pups look on, squealing, "Mommy! Mommy!"

or,

B. You are tied down and at the mercy of a chimpanzee with pliers, who's convinced there's a banana up your nose.

9. How much do you Love Thy Neighbor?

A. You lose a $5,000 bet on the Superbowl;

or,

B. You win the bet, but your next-door neighbor gets abducted and brutally sodomized by devil worshippers.

10. MEN ONLY: How deep is the quality of mercy and forgiveness in you?

A. Either you become nauseous for 30 seconds;

or,

B. The last woman who rejected you gets her tongue butterflied by a mentally disturbed sushi chef?

How You Stack Up

6. Send California into the sea: 64%

   ... *or* take a red-hot needle in the eye: 36%.

7. Send your best friend to prison for a murder he/she did not commit: 32%

   ... *or* submerge your foot in boiling hot water for five full minutes: 68%.

8. Cause a seal to be beaten to death while its pups look on, squealing, "Mommy! Mommy!": 86%

   ... *or* be tied down while facing a chimpanzee with pliers who's convinced a banana lurks deep within your nose: 14%.

9. Lose $5,000 on the Superbowl: 50%

   ... *or* win, but have your neighbor brutally sodomized: 50%.

(NOTE: For a small fee SMITH AND DOE will release the addresses of these 50% for the sake of their neighbors.)

10. Become briefly nauseous: 71%

   ... *or* send the last person who rejected you to have her tongue shredded: 29%.

11. WOMEN ONLY: What is your tolerance for betrayal?   **13**
   A. Your period lasts a week longer than usual;
or,
   B. The last guy who dumped you has all the hair painfully ripped out of his head and replaced with implants of pubic hair from someone of a different race?

12. When push comes to shove, how loyal are you?
   A. The person who gave you your start in business is burned all over his/her body with a lit cigar;
or,
   B. You lose out to your archrival for the job of CEO?

13. How much do you hate to be uncomfortable?
   A. You are forced to fill your mouth with Tabasco sauce (while suffering from an open canker sore) and swish it around for ten minutes;
or,
   B. A vagrant who lives in Guatemala is hit on the head by a falling tree, trapped underneath it, and dies of starvation?

14. How inspired are you by the climbers who survived the recent Mount Everest disaster?
   A. Both your hands are sliced up by razors, then you plunge them into a tub of saltwater and vinegar for five full minutes;
or,
   B. All of the climbers who bravely survived and/or were rescued are trapped on the mountain and die?

15. How tolerant are you of pain?
   A. You must cut off your nose with a hacksaw with no pain killer of any sort;
or,
   B. Half of Congress inhale anthrax spores and die hideously painful deaths moments later?

How You Stack Up

11. Your period lasts a week longer than usual: 25%
... *or* replace a cad's hair with pubes from another race: 75%.

12. Burn your career mentor with a lit cigar: 35%
... *or* lose out to your archrival for the CEO job: 65%.

13. Fill your mouth with Tabasco and swish: 61%
... *or* let a vagrant die an untimely death:39%.

14. Slice your hands and plunge them in vinegar: 55%
... *or* the Mount Everest climbers die on the mountain 45%

15. Cut off your nose with a hacksaw: 59%
... *or* let half of Congress die painfully: 41%.

16. How tolerant did you say you were?

A. Allow a hooded man to amputate one of your fingers with a dirty, not-so-sharp dinner knife;

or,

B. Your best friend gets kidnapped, tied up, and whipped until his/her back is completely bloody and is then released?

17. We haven't talked about your parents in a while . . .

A. Allow a medieval executioner to forcibly pull one of your eyes out of its socket, tear it from the nerves, juggle it, and throw it in the garbage;

or,

B. Your mother or father gets skin cancer, with a 10% chance of recovery?

18. How bothered are you by Fred Goldman's son's horrible death at the (alleged) hands of O. J.?

A. Stick your hand into the garbage disposal while it is running, inevitably mangling it;

or,

B. Fred Goldman's daughter also gets brutally murdered by O. J., and O. J. get off again?

19. How bothered did you say you were?

A. You lose your right leg in a boating accident;

or,

B. Fred Goldman, while mourning the deaths of both his son and daughter at the hands of O. J., also gets murdered by O. J. and O. J. gets off yet again.

20. How brave are you?

A. Slit a vein in your leg and swim for two minutes in shark-infested waters;

or,

B. Allow everyone on your state's death row to get a presidential pardon and reenter society, working for you?

How You Stack Up

16. Amputate your own finger: 13%
    ... *or* send your best friend for a bloody whuppin': 87%.

17. Have your eye yanked out of its socket: 32%
    ... *or* one of your parents contracts skin cancer, most likely fatal: 68%.

18. Mangle your hand in the garbage disposal: 13%
    ... *or* let Fred Goldman's daughter also get murdered by O. J.: 87%.

19. Lose your right leg: 14%
    ... *or* Fred Goldman, while mourning the death of both kids, also gets murdered by O. J.: 86%.

20. Slit a vein and swim with the sharks: 9%
    ... *or* free death row inmates and have them work for you: 91%.

21. How brave did you say you were?

A. Spend ten minutes locked in a steel, windowless cell with a brutal serial rapist/killer whose victims have all resembled you;

or,

B. Condemn every priest and nun on earth to hell for eternity?

22. How much do you revere human freedom?

A. Bear being shut up for 30 days in a three-foot-square box with your own doo-doo, dressed like "the Gimp" in *Pulp Fiction,* while all the jailed dissidents in China are freed forever;

or,

B. Not?

How You Stack Up

21. Spend ten minutes locked in a cell with a brutal rapist/killer whose victims all resemble you: 41%

    ... *or* condemn every priest and nun to hell for eternity: 59%.

22. Sacrifice your freedom for 30 days in order to free all Chinese dissidents: 11%

    ... *or* not: 89%.

The Good News and the Bad News

(You *must* choose one and live with the guilt for the consequences.)

Each of these questions contains some good news and some bad news. When given the choice, don't you only want to hear the good?

1.A. You lose all of your money and are forced to publicly declare Chapter 11 bankruptcy;
or,
B. The pope has a painful heart attack and dies.

2.A. Every person you know receives a check for $10,000,000 from an anonymous benefactor *except you;*
or,
B. *You* receive a check for $250,000.

3.A. *You* get in a bad car accident which puts you in the hospital for a year;
or,
B. Four other people you've never met get in a car accident and die in the burning wreck, leaving eight children without parents, money, or shelter.

20 **How You Stack Up**

1. Lose all your money and declare Chapter 11 bankruptcy: 15%

   ... or let the pope croak: 85%.

2. All your friends get $1,000,000 except you: 54%

   ... or you get $250,000 all to yourself: 46%.

3. You have a car accident but survive: 46%

   ... or four strangers die in car accidents, leaving their children penniless and parentless: 54%.

4.A. Your child is born with a genetic birth defect that
causes one of its legs to be half the size of the other;
or;
B. Your child is born in perfect health, but twenty other
couples will have the same birth defect on their next
child.

☺ ☺ ☺

5.A. You must spend the next thirty days doing sit-ups all
day and night with only three hours of sleep a night;
or;
B. A prison riot will erupt in Nairobi, killing 30 inmates
and 3 guards?

☺ ☺ ☺

6.A. You get caught by U.S. Customs not declaring a
valuable piece of jewelry and face criminal charges that
could result in up to 3 months in prison but will probably
only result in probation;
or;
B. You get away with it, but the young guy behind you
who would have gotten away scott free gets caught with
a roach on the bottom of his bag, is arrested, put in
prison, and becomes a love slave for the Aryan
Brotherhood?

☺ ☺ ☺

7.A. You get an incurable goiter on your neck that looks
like you tried to swallow a squirrel;
or;
B. Your doctor is bitten by a squirrel and dies from a
horrible seizure brought on by rabies.

How You Stack Up

4. Your child is born with different sized legs: 31%.
   ... or twenty couples you don't know have children born with the same leg defect: 69%.

5. You spend the next thirty days doing sit-ups: 38%.
   ... or thirty complete strangers die in a Nairobi prison riot: 62%.

6. You get caught by customs and wind up on probation: 30%
   ... or some poor kid goes to jail: 70%.

7. You get a goiter on your neck: 8%
   ... or your doctor dies from rabid squirrel bite: 92%.

8.A. You lose your wallet with your driver's license, credit cards, and $500 cash;

or,

B. A good samaritan finds and returns your wallet but gets hit by a car on his way home and loses the use of his left hand.

☺ ☺ ☺

9.A. Three guys jump out of a dark alley and beat you to within an inch of your life;

or,

B. Three men jump out of a dark alley and beat your mate's mother to within an inch of her life.

☺ ☺ ☺

10.A. An asteroid crashes into the earth, killing all human life except for you, your family, and your friends;

or,

B. Everyone you have ever met except your family and your friends commits suicide.

☺ ☺ ☺

11.A. You and your mate are visiting the Sphinx and the pyramids when Israel and Egypt declare war;

or,

B. A terrorist detonates a nuclear bomb in Little Rock, Arkansas.

☺ ☺ ☺

12.A. Using all your cash reserves, you just bought a new luxury automobile that turns out to be a total lemon and breaks down every time you drive it out of the service department;

or,

B. 30 illegal immigrants crossing the U.S.A. border in a van are blown to smithereens by a 30-millimeter howitzer shell fired by border police.

Smith *and* Doe

24 **How You Stack Up**

8. You lose your wallet: 92%

   ... *or* a good samaritan gets run over: 8%.

9. You get beaten to within an inch of your life: 45%

   ... *or* your mate's mother gets beaten to within an inch of her life: 55%.

10. An asteroid kills everyone except you, your family, and your friends: 42%

   ... *or* everyone you have ever met (with the exception of the above) commits suicide: 58%.

11. You are in Egypt when a war breaks out: 50%

   ... *or* a terrorist detonates a nuclear bomb in Little Rock, Arkansas: 50%.

12. You buy a luxury car that turns out to be a lemon: 58%

   ... *or* 30 illegal immigrants perish: 42%.

How Much Would You Pay?

In this series of questions, we test your level of selfless compassion by asking . . .

HOW MUCH WOULD YOU ACTUALLY, GENUINELY, HONESTLY PAY *OUT OF YOUR OWN POCKET RIGHT THIS VERY MINUTE* for the following, assuming you would do it anonymously and never take credit for it?

1. Stevie Wonder to regain his sight?

2. World hunger to come to an end for a week?

3. World hunger to come to an end *forever?*

4. To prevent a meteor collision that will destroy the earth 1,000 years after you die?

5. Ensure that your worst enemy will actually go to HELL?

6. For your boss to be guaranteed perfect health for five years?

7. For your best friend to win the Publisher's Clearing House Sweepstakes (therefore making you a pauper in comparison)?

8. Undo 500,000 deaths from World War II?

9. Prevent one of your coworker's from getting in an accident that will cost him or her a leg?

How You Stack Up

	$0	$1–$100	$101–$500	$501–$1,000	$1,001–10,000	$10,0001 AND UP	"All I own"
1.	36%	50%	5%	5%	4%	0%	0%
2.	41%	36%	14%	0%	4%	0%	5%
3.	14%	9%	9%	18%	14%	18%	18%
4.	50%	23%	9%	4%	9%	0%	5%
5.	50%	14%	15%	0%	5%	16%	0%
6.	74%	4%	5%	5%	8%	0%	4%
7.	41%	33%	8%	5%	9%	0%	4%
8.	62%	13%	0%	4%	13%	8%	0%
9.	45%	21%	8%	4%	13%	9%	0%

1. Comments: $20: "Once he saw his girlfriend, he would kill himself, so it's better he remain blind."
$10,000: "Glad to oblige. I've enjoyed his music for years."
$0: "The utter shock of seeing what his corn-rowed hair looks like would cause him to go into cardiac arrest."

2. Comments: $0: "A week of good food would only serve to enrage the starving masses."
$1,000: "Sally Struthers would be out of a job."
$0: "Let them eat each other."

3. Comments: $——: "All my money. Anyone who doesn't is an asshole."
$0: "I'm still waiting for another Band-Aid concert."
$500: "It's all I have."

4. Comments: $0: "I'll be dead. So will my immediate family and offspring, so who cares?"
$5: "Which, after 1,000 years of compounded interest, will be a lot of $."
$0: "Fuck 'em."

5. Comments: $5,000: "Coach, not business class."
$0: "But I'd pay $5,000 to watch the chimpanzee with pliers look for the banana up their nose."
$0: "He'll wind up there on his own."

6. Comments: $0: "For bad health, that's another story."
- $200: "Yes, that is a negative sign."
$All the money I have: "My boss is my mom."

7. Comments: $100: "Hopefully I'd be spoiled by the friend with her winnings."
$260: "Maybe the cocksucker will reimburse me or at least take me out to dinner."
$25: "Just to see how badly it fucks him up."

8. Comments: $0: "It would screw up the time-space continuum."
$0: "I loved WWII."
$10,000: "But only to save the Jews."

9. Comments: $20: "More if I'm presently fucking the girl."
$0: "Isn't that the company's responsibility?"
$0: "It might double my workload."

10. To prevent one of your coworker's from losing an eye?

11. To prevent one of your coworkers from losing *both* eyes?

12. To personally avoid all sexually transmitted diseases for the rest of your life, even if you never wear protection?

13. For the eradication of STDs from the face of the earth?

14. To cure every AIDS patient fully and immediately?

15. To become world famous?

16. To become president of the United States?

17. To free innocent prisoners from jails the world over?

18. To keep a 16-year-old girl from becoming pregnant?

19. To see the pope naked?

20. To see Saddam Hussein naked?

21. To see Bill Clinton naked?

How You Stack Up

$0	$1–$100	$101–$500	$501–$1,000	$1,001–$10,000	$10,001 AND UP	"All I own"
10. 49%	21%	4%	8%	9%	5%	4%

Comments: $500: "How bad would you feel if you could do something and didn't?"
$0: "Eye patch jokes would be good comedy."

$0	$1–$100	$101–$500	$501–$1,000	$1,001–$10,000	$10,001 AND UP	"All I own"
11. 45%	21%	9%	5%	12%	8%	0%

Comments: $500: "But let's not push it" (from same person who said $500 above).
$25: "May impact business negatively."
$10,000: "$5,000 each."

$0	$1–$100	$101–$500	$501–$1,000	$1,001–$10,000	$10,001 AND UP	"All I own"
12. 41%	4%	9%	8%	8%	25%	5%

Comments: $25,000: "I'd save that much on condoms alone."
$5,000: "Paradise."

$0	$1–$100	$101–$500	$501–$1,000	$1,001–$10,000	$10,001 AND UP	"All I own"
13. 54%	8%	4%	9%	3%	18%	4%

Comments: $0: "That's population control for minorities."
$0: "I spent my money on the last question and I'm now STD-free forever, so who cares?"
$5,000: "Women would much more readily hook and swallow."

$0	$1–$100	$101–$500	$501–$1,000	$1,001–$10,000	$10,001 AND UP	"All I own"
14. 43%	27%	0%	0%	8%	13%	7%

Comments: $1,000,000: "I would only want hemophiliacs and homosexuals cured. Drug users deserve it."
$—: "Life savings. Even borrow from the bank."
$0: "Don't want to play God."

$0	$1–$100	$101–$500	$501–$1,000	$1,001–$10,000	$10,001 AND UP	"All I own"
15. 40%	5%	4%	4%	30%	5%	12%

Comments: $10,000: "More chicks."
$1,000: "Hopefully I'll make it all back plus more from endorsements."
$0: "Hitler was world famous. So was Kurt Cobain. The price of fame can be high enough without paying for it up front."

$0	$1–$100	$101–$500	$501–$1,000	$1,001–$10,000	$10,001 AND UP	"All I own"
16. 87%	0%	0%	0%	9%	4%	0%

Comments: $10,000: "Twenty if Lewinsky's still there."
$0: "Who wants that suckass $200,000-a-year job?"
$0: "You wouldn't want me as president."

$0	$1–$100	$101–$500	$501–$1,000	$1,001–$10,000	$10,001 AND UP	"All I own"
17. 43%	26%	0%	6%	8%	9%	8%

Comments: $0: "After you release them, they will be as disturbed as if they were guilty inmates."
$200: "Goes up to $2,000,000 if it happens to be me."
$10,000: "Unjust suffering is hell on earth."

18. 53%   21%   5%   0%   8%   9%   4%
Comments: $10: "To buy a box of condoms."
          $0: "Did that already."
          $250: "Too many people on earth already."

19. 79%   16%   5%   0%   0%   0%   0%
Comments: $0: "Who wants to see that 78-year-old uncircumcised crane?"
          $All of my money: " . . . to be spared the sight!"
          $500: "Would pay more, but may piss God off."

20. 74%   26%   0%   0   0%   0%   0%
Comments: $100: "I'd like to see how hairy and sweaty those nuts are."
          $1: "His schlong always points toward Mecca."
          $0: "Naked *and dead* . . . all my money!"

21. 100%   0%   0   0%   0%   0%   0%
Comments: $0: "I don't have to see him, I can just ask any female intern who's worked
          for him in the last six years."
          $0: "Used goods."
          $0: "I'm sure pics will surface for free soon enough."

22. MEN: How much would you pay *Hustler* magazine to let you:
  Shoot a nude pictorial of the Spice Girls?

23. . . . of Elle MacPherson?

24. . . . and you happen to look exactly like her dream guy?

☺ ☺ ☺

25. WOMEN: How much would you pay to shoot a *Playgirl* layout of Brat Pitt and immediately go to dinner with him afterwards?

☺ ☺ ☺

Assuming you could get it back for free, how much would you pay to:

26. Lose your pinky ring inside Heather Locklear?

27. Condemn your ex-mate to never be found attractive by the opposite sex ever again?

☺ ☺ ☺

What's your top offer to:

28. Release a putrid fart in a crowded elevator and have everyone think it's the woman beside you?

29. Smack your mate in the face so hard he/she blacks out and doesn't remember it?

30. Cheat the IRS and make them think the cheater wasn't you but your worst enemy?

31. Turn your boss into Janet Reno's gynecologist?

How You Stack Up

$0	$1–$100	$101–$500	$501–$1,000	$1,001–$10,000	$10,001 and up	"All I own"

22. 51% 26% 8% 6% 9% 0% 0%

Comments: $——: "Would have to get a calculator out for that one."
$20: "If it included a blow job."
$0: "I'm sick of them."

23. 44% 13% 19% 6% 14% 4% 0%

Comments: $19.95: "(The price of a one-year subscription to *Hustler*.)"
$25: "($2.00 per hot spot)."
$1,000: "If it's all I can eat."

24. 0% 17% 6% 54% 11% 11% 0%

Comments: $150,000: "Plus all my money for the next two years."
$750: "More if I can slip her a roofie too."
$25: "Real or bootleg?"

25. 2% 8% 42% 8% 28% 10% 2%

Comments: $500: "For John Jr. in his Calvins!"
$1,000: "The man is a God."
$0: "He looks like my ex-husband."

26. 52% 21% 5% 6% 12% 4% 0%

Comments: $100,000: "Just to stick my fingers in her would be worth it: she can keep the ring."
$15: "Inside which orifice?"
$0: "Who wears a pinky ring?"

27. 22% 17% 45% 6% 0% 0% 0%

Comments: $100: "A bargain for a lifetime of torture."
$0: "Too harsh a punishment, even for him."
$0: "Why pay for something that's already reality?"

28. 26% 51% 11% 12% 0% 0% 0%

Comments: $250: "Especially if we are going to the penthouse in a 100-story building."
$10: "I do this for nothing every day."
$100: "As long as I can claim the $100 as an 'entertainment' business deduction."

29. 62% 16% 5% 6% 11% 0% 0%

Comments: $500: "A moment to cherish forever."
$100. "I've always wanted to hit someone and not suffer the consequences."
$0: "Why pay when I get to do it for free?"
$0: "An elephant never forgets."
$3,000: "Overdue."

30. 39% 13% 26% 7% 6% 9% 0%

Comments: $1,000: "How satisfying is this!?"
$10,000: "If I can cheat big time."
$500: "(The amount I typically pay.)"

31. 58% 23% 6% 7% 0% 0% 6%

Comments: $100: "What a vile thought!"
$1,000: "The problem is he might like it."
$0: "Not even my boss deserves that."

Keeping in mind your highly developed humanitarian in- **33**
stincts, how much would you be willing to pay to:

32. Have personally brought Chris Farley back to life through mouth-to-mouth resuscitation?

33. How about Mama Cass? (Keeping in mind she was choking on her own vomit at the time.)

34. Marilyn Monroe? (Assuming you first get to remove the Seconal suppository with your tongue.)

☺ ☺ ☺

What is your bottom-line offer to:
35. Arrest and convict Jon Benet's killer?

36. See O. J. Simpson get slowly tortured to death by Fred Goldman?

☺ ☺ ☺

What would you actually pay to know:
37. Exactly what your mate was thinking at the moment of his/her last climax?

38. Your mate's favorite most frequently occurring sexual fantasy?

39. The name of the worst person your mate has ever gone to bed with, the one who mysteriously dropped off his/her résumé?

How You Stack Up

$0	$1–$100	$101–$500	$501–$1,000	$1,001–$10,000	$10,001 and up	"All I own"
32. 47%	29%	4%	6%	12%	0%	2%

Comments: $0: "Wouldn't pay but I'd love to still have him around."
$100: "Do I get a reward?"
$———: "All my money to be spared the task!"

33. 63%	13%	6%	5%	8%	4%	1%

Comments: $0: "Are you a fan of vomit?"
$0: "Who cares when there is still Wilson Phillips?"
$100: "Only if I'm guaranteed to get a few big chunks in my mouth."

34. 23%	35%	12%	8%	7%	11%	4%

Comments: $500: "I'd love the chance to literally kiss ass with a legend."
$0: "But I wouldn't mind dabbling in a little necrophelia."
$2,650: "Liked her $150 more than Chris Farley or Mama Cass."

35. 48%	19%	9%	4%	8%	4%	0%

Comments: $50: "She was hot!"
$50,000: "Banking on recouping my investment on a book deal."
$0: "Who's Jon Benet?"

36. 45%	36%	9%	6%	4%	0%	0%

Comments: $0: "I'd rather spend my money to see him get caught and used as a sex toy in prison."
$75: "Only if I get to keep the Bronco."
$0: "But it would make a damn good *Saturday Night Live* skit."

37. 59%	18%	14%	9%	0%	0%	0%

Comments: $200: "I'm not sure if I want to know, but it's too tempting to resist."
$50: "It's probably too depressing."
$1: "I'm sure it was. 'I can't believe the size of that massive crane!' "

38. 54%	14%	12%	18%	2%	0%	0%

Comments: $100: "I can probably guess it involves two women, not including myself."
$500: "I'd make it happen frequently."
$0: "Unfortunately for me, I already know."

39. 72%	13%	10%	5%	0%	0%	0%

Comments: $250: "As long as it isn't me!"
$100: "Good for when big argument comes. Nice to have ammo."
$0: "I'm no masochist."

40. How much of a raise your boss would be willing, if nailed to the wall, to give you?

41. How much would you pay for a video of your mate engaged in his/her most erotic past experience?

☺ ☺ ☺

Assuming you ran into a genuine genie (who refused to work for free), what is the most you would spend to:

42. Have the power to instantly hypnotize cheerleaders?

43. Be the sexiest girl in your office?

☺ ☺ ☺

How much would you pay right this moment to:

44. MEN: Have Monica Lewinsky show up at your house, give you the best blow job of your life, and then turn around and leave? (You'll have to pay extra for her to keep it a secret.)

45. WOMEN: Have Brad Pitt appear, perform oral sex on you until orgasm, and then turn around and leave? (You'll have to pay extra for him to stay.)

46. Have the power to make anyone do anything you want simply by telling them to do it (and do it with a smile on their face)?

Smith
and
Doe

How You Stack Up

	$0	$1–$100	$101–$500	$501–$1,000	$1,001–$10,000	$10,001 and up	"All I own"
40.	63%	9%	4%	6%	18%	0%	0%

Comments: $———: "Three-forths of whatever the raise would be."
$100: "Just to see them squirm."
$5,000: "I'm worth at least that."

	$0						
41.	84%	6%	3%	7%	0%	0%	0%

Comments: $1,000: "Plus free barf bag."
$0: "I have it on tape already, and I'm in it!"
$0: "But I'd pay $5,000 if it was with another girl."

	$0						
42.	44%	13%	6%	7%	14%	12%	0%

Comments: $0: "They are pretty easy to hyponotize without a genie."
$3 of my net worth: "Dallas, here I come!"
$500: "Zero at the Citadel."

	$0						
43.	73%	19%	8%	0%	0%	0%	0%

Comments: $0: "I already am."
$0: "Unless it would help me get a promotion."
$0: "There are no men in my office."

	$0						
44.	56%	19%	13%	8%	4%	0%	0%

Comments: $1,000: "Great for the résumé."
$10: "She'd have to hum 'Hail to the Chief' to get any more."
$500: "If it's the best head of my life, who cares who is performing it?"

	$0						
45.	74%	21%	5%	0%	0%	0%	0%

Comments: $0: "Not my type."
$100: "$100 more for him to stay two hours."
$10,000: "My hidden video will be worth a lot more than that to the *Enquirer.*"

	$0						
46.	0%	0%	0%	0%	0%	0%	100%

Comments: $:All I have.
$:Everything I own.
$:My entire net worth.

*As every successful business person knows, the profitable
thing is not always the right thing. Nobody ever made money
by insisting on doing the right thing. Here are some things
that are not-so-right, extremely not-so-right, and horrifically
not-so-right—but they're all money makers. As the man in
the cut-rate clothing commercial says . . .*

"Money Talks, Nobody Walks"

(Each of the following involves three different business propositions. You must choose one.)

1. For **$5,000**, which would you do:
 A. Renounce your religion on public access TV.
 B. Expose your genitals in the busiest part of Beverly Hills;
 or,
 C. Eat a small cat turd in Macy's window?

2. For **$10,000**, which would you do:
 A. Walk around all day with a large, oysterlike booger hanging from your nose (which you cannot explain to anyone);
 B. Suck all the snot from the nose of a business associate who has a cold (which you may then spit out);
 or,
 C. Stick your nose against the anus of a platonic friend (and keep it there for three full minutes)?

3. For **$50,000**, which would you do:
 A. Take a full dump (including wiping) while on office-wide closed-circuit TV;
 B. Masturbate and achieve climax in front your boss;
 or,
 C. Seriously ask every single person in your company how to best get the skid marks out of your underwear?

How You Stack Up

1. For **$5,000:**
   Renounce your religion: 50%;
   expose your genitals: 38%;
   or eat a small cat turd: 12%.

2. For **$10,000:**
   Walk around with a huge booger hanging: 71%;
   eat someone's noseful of snot: 2%;
   or stick your own nose in platonic friend's butt: 27%.

3. For **50,000:**
   Take a dump on office-wide TV: 12%;
   masturbate in front of your boss:0%;
   or ask advice on underwear skid mark removal: 88%.

4. For **$100,000**, which would you do:

A. Jump naked into a Dumpster of dead, mutilated hamsters from a second-story window (assuming you would not be injured);

B. Wearing no gloves or mask, dispose of a week-old cadaver after a botched autopsy;

or,

C. See how far you can work a plumber's snake up your own rectum? (A SMITH AND DOE representative must validate your effort.)

5. For **$500,000**, which would you do:

A. Adopt Siamese twins joined at the neck;

B. Adopt a three-legged boy;

or,

C. Adopt a girl with four breasts.

6. For **1,000,000**, which would you do:

A. Marry a quadriplegic;

B. Appear on a telethon to taunt children afflicted with muscular dystrophy;

or,

C. "Accidentally" on purpose run over a panhandler, turning him into a glorified cabbage?

7. For **$10,000,000**, which would you do:

A. Sacrifice a 13-year-old virgin (given, of course, that no one will ever know about it);

B. Strangle your closest relative to within an inch of their life, rendering them comatose for several days (and never be able to explain why you did it);

or,

C. Actually kidnap a seven-year-old child for one week then release him/her with the total security of knowing you'll never get caught?

How You Stack Up

4. For **$100,000:**
Jump naked into dead hamster Dumpster: 44%,
dispose of a bloody cadaver: 44%;
or work a plumber's snake into your butt: 12%.

5. For **500,000:**
Adopt a Siamese twin: 14%,
adopt a three-legged boy: 72%;
or adopt a girl with four breast: 14%.

6. For **$1,000,000:**
Marry a quadriplegic: 14%;
taunt "Jerry's Kids": 29%;
or "accidentally" run over a panhandler: 57%.

7. For **$10,000,000:**
Sacrifice a 13-year-old virgin: 18%;
strangle (but not kill) your closest friend: 48%;
or kidnap an innocent child: 34%.

8. For **$100,000,000**:

A. Horribly maim and disfigure your father or mother?

B. Horribly maim and disfigure your sister or brother?

or,

C. Horribly maim and disfigure yourself?

(Note: For A or B you may consult with those to be maimed and disfigured in order to split up the prize money in a fair and equitable manner.)

How You Stack Up

8. For $100,000,000:
Maim and disfigure your father or
mother: 12%,
Maim and disfigure your sister or
brother: 25%;
or, Maim and disfigure yourself:
63%.

Sex Related

You knew we were coming to this. You can make enough to retire forever right here and all it might take is a deep, long breath. Some of these acts may seem revolting on the surface, but when you really think about them, the worst that can happen is you risk your life (plus, it can't be as bad as that guy/girl you hooked up with after all that Tequila in college). But the fact is, you risk your life every day when you get in a car, ski a slope, smoke a cigarette, and not only do you do those for free, you pay to do them. So, if you're not risking your life, what is the worst you are doing? Something that merely nauseates you to the very core? You've thrown up for nothing in the past, this time we're offering good hard cash for blowing a few chunks. Tell the truth: You'd do it, wouldn't you?

(Payment amount: Horrific sex act required for payment.)

1. $100,000 **(MEN OR WOMEN):** Give Rush Limbaugh a blow job (no swallowing required).

2. $250,000: Same as above, except he's got a reddish sore on his penis.

3. $50,000 **(MEN OR WOMEN):** Perform oral sex on Rosanne Barr at her fattest, after she has spent three days working out and hasn't showered.

4. $75,000: Same as above, except she has a yeast infection.

5. $100,000: Same as above, except she's also got crabs.

6. $500,000: Same as above, except she has a yeast infection, crabs, and she's having the heaviest period of her life.

How You Stack Up

1. 24% would give Rush Limbaugh a blow job.

2. 14% would do it with a reddish sore on his penis.

3. 38% would do oral sex on Rosanne Barr.

4. 23% would do it when she has a yeast infection . . .

5. . . . and crabs: 17% . . .

6. . . . a yeast infection, crabs, and the worst period of her life (known as "the combination plate"): 26%.

7. **$150,000: MEN:** You will be unable to attain so much as a partial erection for the next year. **HETEROSEXUAL WOMEN:** No man you are sexually involved with will be able to get so much as a partial erection for the next year. **LESBIAN WOMEN:** Your tongue will be unable to function in any other capacity than to aid in speech and eating, nor will the tongue of anyone you become involved with for the next year.

☺ ☺ ☺

8. **$50,000,000, GUYS ONLY.** A nude prostitute stands in front of you. The good news is she is stunningly gorgeous. The bad news is that she hasn't had an AIDS test in ten years. All you have to do to get the $50 mil is to have anal sex with her for 5 seconds WITH NO CONDOM. That's right, only 5 seconds. That works out to $10,000,000 per second. Would you do it?

9. **$100,000,000:** Same as above, except with a Haitian prostitute.

10. **$200,000,000:** Same as above, except with a Haitian prostitute and with a small, bleeding nick on your penis.

☺ ☺ ☺

11. **$30,000:** A random person walking down the street will be placed nude in a windowless room in the middle of nowhere. You are required to walk in the room, lick the person's sphincter three times, and leave. The person will have just showered and there is no risk of any inadequate wiping. The person will never see your face.

Smith
and
Doe

46 **How You Stack Up**

7. No sexual activity for an entire year: Men: 44%, Women: 76%.

8. 62% would have 5 seconds of unprotected anal sex with an untested prostitute.

9. . . . make that a *Haitian* prostitute: 30%.

10. . . . with a small, bleeding nick on their penis: 0%.

11. 57% would lick a random person's sphincter three times.

(SMITH AND DOE are aghast at what 57% of you will do for a lowball figure.)

12. $50,000: Same as above, except the person hasn't showered.

13. $150,000: Same as above, except the person just had diarrhea but wiped as adequately as they could.

☺ ☺ ☺

14. $1,000,000: **MEN ONLY.** Put your penis in the vagina of a month-old corpse. You only need to put it in to the hilt and then pull it out and you get paid.

☺ ☺ ☺

15. $500,000: **MEN ONLY:** You must have sex with a sheep for one minute of full thrusting.

16. $750,000: Same as above, except you must have an orgasm inside the sheep or you receive nothing.

17. $5,000,000: You must perform oral sex on the sheep until the sheep has an orgasm (and a SMITH AND DOE–approved, certified veterinarian must confirm an orgasm took place).

18. $5,000,000: No sex required, but you must actually insert your head into the anus of the sheep up to your neck. You may need to talk dirty to it for some time before getting it really relaxed.

☺ ☺ ☺

19. $250,000: **WOMEN ONLY:** You must give Al Sharpton a blow job.

20. $350,000: Same as above, except you must swallow. He will provide proof of a recent AIDS test.

How You Stack Up

12. . . . except the person hasn't showered: 38%.

13. . . . and the person just had diarrhea: 34%.

14. 61% will have sex with a corpse.

15. 69% will do it with sheep,

16. . . . and have an orgasm inside the sheep: 49%,

17. . . . or have oral sex with the sheep until orgasm: 32%.

18. 50% will put their head into a sheep's butt up to their neck.

19. 60% will give Al Sharpton a blow job.

20. . . . and swallow: 67%.

21. $500,000: Same as above, except this one's for hetero-sexual men.

22. $2,000,000; WOMEN ONLY (we urge you to answer *honestly*): With a guarantee of no AIDS, would you give a random person off the street a blow job without ever so much as speaking to them? You are guaranteed not to know them, with no common acquaintances, and you will never see them again and you MUST swallow.

23. $3,000,000: Same as above, except you must also have sex with them.

☺ ☺ ☺

24. $5,000, WOMEN ONLY: You walk into a room and there is a nude man with a bag over his head. You are re-quired to walk over to him and lick the sweaty underside of his testicles 3 times. You may then leave and get paid.

25. $15,000, MEN ONLY: Same thing, except you must ac-tually put his penis in your mouth until it becomes fully erect, which, if he's a normal man, will take all of about 3 seconds.

☺ ☺ ☺

26. $50,000: You must perform oral sex on your best friend of the opposite sex until orgasm. You may discuss this with him/her and share the payment if you so desire.

27. $100,000: Same as above, except sex is required.

28. $300,000: Same as above, except anal sex is required.

How You Stack Up

21. . . . same, except for heterosexual men: 50%.

22. 33% will give a random person a blow job.

23. . . . same as above, except have sex with them and a lot of extra$: 50%.

24. 80% will lick the underside of a random guy's sweaty testicles.

25. . . . except this one's for men, and you have to put his penis in your mouth until he becomes erect: 6%.

26. 82% would have oral sex with your best friend of the opposite sex until orgasm. (Apparently there are those who will do this for free.)

27. . . . except you must copulate too: 95%. (Even more want to go all the way.)

28. . . . except you must also have anal sex: 76%. (A distinct fall-off in numbers.)

29. $1,000,000: Same as above, except you must do it with your best friend of the same sex.

☺ ☺ ☺

30. $100,000, **MEN ONLY:** There are 10 gorgeous nude women in front of you. One of them has AIDS, the others are disease free. You must perform oral scx on only one of them for 5 minutes in order to get paid.

31. $250,000: Same as above, except all 10 women are having their periods.

32. $500,000: Same as above, except their periods are especially heavy.

☺ ☺ ☺

33. $10,000: Play a naked background extra in a hard-core porn movie.

34. $20,000: Play a naked, nonsexual, *speaking* role in a hard-core porn film, with your real name in the credits.

35. $30,000: Demonstrate the use of a lifelike butt plug in a porn film.

☺ ☺ ☺

36. $1,000,000: Bend over, spread your cheeks, and smile at the camera for the cover of *BUTTHOLE* magazine (men only get $1,000).

☺ ☺ ☺

37. $5,000: Wedge a mature butternut squash in your vagina.

38. $10,000: Carry a cucumber in your vagina for an entire day.

How You Stack Up

29. ... except with your best friend of the same sex: 24%.

30. 52% will take their chances performing oral sex on a group of women, *one of whom* has AIDS.

31. ... and they are all having their periods: 36%.

32. ... and their periods are especially heavy: 34%.

33. 62% would play a naked background extra in a porn movie.

34. 53% would play a nonsexual speaking role in a porn movie.

35. Only 19% would demonstrate the use of a butt plug on film.

36. 68% would wink their eye and their sphincter at the camera for the cover of *BUTTHOLE* magazine.

37. 60% would wedge a butternut squash in their vagina.

38. 61% would carry a cucumber in their vagina for an entire day.

39. $20,000: Same as above, but tell your friends you have a cucumber in your vagina.

40. $25,000: Same as above, but tell your boss you have a cucumber in your vagina.

☺ ☺ ☺

41. $10,000: Copulate (with a condom) with a six-hundred-pound individual who possesses a nice personality.

42. $25,000: Copulate with a six-hundred-pound Samoan.

43. $50,000: Copulate with an angry six-hundred-pound Samoan.

44. $100,000: Copulate with either a six-hundred-pound screaming gay, cross-dressing male, or a six-hundred-pound jack-booted lesbian.

45. $250,000: Copulate with a six-hundred-pound moron who has never been potty-trained, with a tendency to empty his bowels when excited.

46. $1,000,000: Copulate with a six-hundred-pound toothless hillbilly in a shotgun-shack outhouse.

How You Stack Up

39. . . . but you must also tell your friends the cucumber is in your vagina: 65%.

40. . . . and tell your boss: 33%.

41. 50% would have sex with a 600-pound nice person.

42. . . . with a 600-pound Samoan: 37%.

43. . . . with an angry 600-pound Samoan: 31%.

44. . . . with a 600-pound cross-dresser/jack-booted lesbian: 37%.

45. . . . with a 600-pound retard: 4%.

46. . . . with a 600-pound toothless hillbilly in an outhouse (but for lots more$): 31%.

"Bargain Basement"

We're practically giving away money here. These are things we're certain you would do for a lot less but we'll take the hit in order to get you hooked on the thrill of having money. Remember, this is not a game—it's a journey of self-discovery, so before you turn up your nose at some of these offers, imagine your closets and drawers overflowing with crisp, new, unmarked Ben Franklins. Measure the delight of the freedom and security that money affords against the annoying moment or two it will take to earn it.

1. $2,500: Shave your head bald. The hair will grow back, but you must attend work as usual and are not allowed to wear any type of hairpiece.

2. $3,500: Same as above, but you must wear a bad, ill-fitting hairpiece.

3. $5,000: Same as above, but with your eyebrows shaven as well.

4. $25,000: Same as above, but with no hairpiece and you must tattoo **"Bestiality Rules"** on your bald head.

5. $2,500: Walk into any random public bathroom and lick one small portion of the seemingly clean toilet seat.

6. $5,000: Lick the same spot, but under the seat.

7. $7,500: Without flushing first, put your head inside the water in the bowl and then flush.

8. $10,000: Remove the urinal puck from the urinal in a public bathroom and lick it clean.

9. $12,500: Take a bite out of the urinal puck.

Smith
and
Doe

56

How You Stack Up

1. Shave your head bald: 38%.

2. ... and wear a bad hairpiece:23%.

3. ... and shave your eyebrows: 31%.

4. ... and tattoo **"Bestiality Rules"** on your head: 23%.

5. Lick the toilet seat: 54%.

6. Lick under the seat: 46%.

7. Put your head in the bowl and flush: 23%.

8. Lick the urinal puck: 15%.

9. Bite the urinal puck: 15%.

10. $15,000: You will be required to chug an eight-ounce glass of urine. The urine is standard urine with nothing hideous about it other than the fact that it is some random person's urine.

11. $20,000: Same as above, except the urine comes from a homeless person.

12. $30,000: Same as above, except you must chug it *directly* from the source.

☺ ☺ ☺

13. $15,000: Chug a randomly selected, eight-ounce glass of vomit (hot or cold, your option).

☺ ☺ ☺

14. $15,000: You must make an anonymous bomb threat to the White House from a phone located within walking distance of the White House itself.

15. $25,000: Same as above, except you must stay on the line for two full minutes before hanging up.

☺ ☺ ☺

16. $5,000: Set fire to an abandoned building, assuming no one will get hurt.

17. $10,000: Set fire to an abandoned building with a convicted child molester sleeping in it. (The molester has served time, but 95% of child molesters are repeat offenders.)

18. $10: Set fire to an abandoned building with O. J. sleeping in it.

How You Stack Up

10. Chug a glass of urine: 13%.

11. ... from a homeless person: 8%.

12. ... straight from the penis of a homeless person: 8%.

13. Chug a glass of vomit: 10%.

14. Make a bomb threat to the White House: 8%.

15. ... and stay on the line for two minutes before hanging up: 0%.

16. Set fire to an abandoned building: 62%.

17. ... with a convicted child molestor sleeping in it: 62%.

18. ... with O. J. sleeping in it: 40%.

19. $1,500: Shoot a *Hustler* pictorial of Janet Reno.

20. $5,000: Same as above, but you must shoot the photos within smelling distance.

☺ ☺ ☺

21. $599: Release a *silent*, putrid fart in a crowded elevator.

22. $1,599: Release a *loud*, putrid fart in a crowded elevator.

23. $3,000: Release a loud, putrid fart in a crowded elevator and proudly say, "Take a whiff of that beaut!"

☺ ☺ ☺

24. $5,000: Run across the diameter of Central Park completely nude.

25. $10,000: Same as above, except you must repeat at the top of your lungs, "Viva la France! Viva la France!" throughout the run.

☺ ☺ ☺

26. $5,000: Go to a restaurant, have a great meal with great service, and then call the manager over and file a totally fabricated complaint about how horrible the service was, as your hapless server looks on in shock and confusion?

27. $15,000: Same as above, except you must swear out a claim that your waiter/waitress sexually harassed you as well.

28. $25,000: Same as above, except you only get paid if the waiter/waitress actually gets fired on the spot.

How You Stack Up

19. Shoot a *Hustler* pictorial of Janet Reno: 54%.

20. . . . within smelling distance: 45%.

21. Release a *silent,* putrid fart in an elevator: 62%.

22. Release a *loud,* putrid fart in an elevator: 45%.

23. . . . and yell, "Take a whiff of that beaut!": 54%.

24. Run across Central Park completely nude: 23%.

25. . . . while yelling "Viva la France! Viva la France!": 24%.

26. Frame your server for horrible service: 62%.

27. . . . and sexual harrassment: 25%.

28. . . . plus get them fired on the spot: 23%.

29. $5,000 **(HETEROSEXUAL MEN ONLY):** Go to a gay bar and sit at the bar by yourself from 6:00 P.M. until closing.

30. $10,000 **(HETEROSEXUAL MEN ONLY):** Same as above, except you must pretend to be gay and engage in conversation with anyone who wishes to speak to you.

31. $25,000 **(HETEROSEXUAL MEN ONLY):** Allow a photo of yourself to be used in a national campaign for gay cruises.

32. $25,000 **(WOMEN ONLY):** Star in an educational video that explains to young women in graphic detail (using you as the model) the process of inserting and removing a tampon.

33. $25,000 **(MEN ONLY):** Allow a photo of yourself to be used in a national campaign for a penis-enlargement pump.

34. $25,000 **(WOMEN ONLY):** Allow a photo of yourself to be used in a national douche campaign targeting women who smell "putrid."

How You Stack Up

29. **MEN:** Go to a gay bar and sit alone until closing: 46%.

30. ... and pretend you are gay: 38%.

31. **MEN:** Allow a photo of yourself to be used in an ad campaign for gay cruises: 36%.

32. **WOMEN:** Star in an educational video showing in graphic detail the process of inserting and removing a tampon: 0%.

33. **MEN:** allow a photo of yourself to be used in an ad campaign for a penis-enlargement pump: 36%.

34. **WOMEN:** allow a photo of yourself to be used in a douche campaign targeting women who smell "putrid": 0%.

Questions of Personal Ethics

Here you are placed in a hypothetical situation in which you must choose one of two solutions based on the strength of your commitment to your own personal ethics. None of us wants to see or be responsible for the suffering of others, that's true (then again, how hard did you laugh when you watched your friend slip on the ice and slam onto his or her back that time). But all of us feel that we've earned the right to our own comforts and convictions. When it gets right down to it, where do you fit in?

1. You're a card-carrying New York liberal who has lived for 20 years in a comfortable 5-bedroom apartment for which you pay a measly $300 per month due to rent control. You must choose one, would you rather:
    A. 1,000 homeless people receive free food and shelter for a year;
    or,
    B. The legislature kills a pending new law that will abolish rent control?

2. You're a rabid conservative from Iowa who never misses a Right to Life demonstration. Would you rather:
    A. The Supreme Court overturn Roe vs. Wade;
    or,
    B. Your daughter is raped by a roving gang of crack-smoking hip-hoppers. You find the crack-smoking hip-hoppers, torture them to death . . . and get away with it?

3. You're on the hot streak of your life, up $50,000 at a crap table in Vegas. Someone says your husband/wife is on the phone, crying hysterically. His/her mother just got killed in a drive-by shooting. Would you:
    A. Run to the phone and console your spouse;
    or,
    B. Keep rolling the dice?

How You Stack Up

1. 1,000 homeless get food and shelter for a year: 60%
   ... *or* your rent stays low: 40%.

2. The Supreme Court overturns Roe vs. Wade: 14%
   ... *or* you personally obliterate your daughter's rapists: 86%.

3. You console your heartbroken spouse: 57%
   ... *or* keep rolling the dice: 43%.

4. Your mate is a committed supporter of animal rights and you just bought a shiny new black BMW. Every time your car's parked in your driveway, the same cute little bird flies down and pecks at its reflection, chipping away at your shiny new $70,000 paint job. Would you rather:

A. Go to the trouble of hauling out your car cover every single time you park;

or,

B. Pay a neighborhood kid $5 to shoot the bird when you and your mate are away for the day?

5. You're a religious person who worships on Sundays and prays every day. On a business trip, you lock eyes with a gorgeous blonde who is just getting ready to leave the hotel bar. You realize there is only a moment for something to happen. Would you:

A. Pray to God that she finds you irresistible;

or,

B. Slip a roofie in her drink, rendering her wrecked out of her mind and very horny (assuming there is no chance of you getting busted either by her or the authorities)?

6. Your father dies. At the reading of his will, you find that he has left his multimillion-dollar estate to your only sibling, with the provision that when your sibling dies, the fortune passes on to you. Would you rather:

A. Your not-so-beloved sibling lives a long and happy life with your father's money;

or,

B. Plunges into an open manhole and dies upon leaving the lawyer's office?

7. You own a restaurant in which an innocent patron gets a serious case of food poisoning. Would you rather:

A. The victim sues you for a fortune, wins, and eventually recovers their health;

or,

B. Remains in a coma for the rest of their life and never files suit?

How You Stack Up

4. You put the car cover on every time you park: 29%

... *or* pay a guy to kill the damn bird: 71%.

5. You pray to God that the attractive stranger finds you irresistible: 50%

... *or* slip a roofie in her drink with no chance of getting caught: 50%.

6. Your sibling gets the money and lives: 65%

... *or* dies and you get the money: 35%.

7. The victim sues you and wins: 47%

... *or* the victim remains in a coma forever: 53%.

8. It's the day of the Superbowl and you're hoping the Publisher's Clearing House Prize Patrol is about to ring your doorbell with a 10 million check. Remember, you can only pick one. Would you rather:

A. The prize patrol arrives, but as they pay you the $10,000,000, a nuclear terrorist bomb explodes at the game, killing 100,000 total strangers;

or,

B. The bomb doesn't go off and the prize patrol continues on to your neighbor's house, giving him the $10,000,000?

9. You're on an international flight from a Third World country and the plane is packed, not one empty seat. You consider yourself a dignified, tactful person, but the body odor of the guy next to you is literally making you gag. Would you rather:

A. Stand up in the rear of the plane for the whole ten-hour flight?

or,

B. Cause the man to contract a horrible bout of food poisoning, forcing him to spend the full ten hours in the bathroom, painfully, convulsively vomiting the entire time?

10. MEN ONLY: You are an executive of a public company who has cultivated the image of an ethical businessman. Your wife, who is 23, 36-24-36, and gives the world's greatest head, tells you to either make more money or she's leaving. You have the opportunity to make a real killing by illegally sharing highly confidential inside information on your company. Would you:

A. Tell your wife to hit the road;

or,

B. Make the insider trade?

68 How You Stack Up

8. You get the $10 mil but 100,000 strangers get blown to kingdom come: 55%

   ... *or* your next-door neighbor gets the $10 mil: 45%.

9. You have to stand in the rear of the plane: 24%

   ... *or* the foul-smelling Third Worlder gets food poisoning: 76%.

10. You tell your wife to hit the road: 47%

   ... *or* you make the insider trade: 53%.

11. WOMEN ONLY: You and your mate have been together for years and are truly in love. Then you meet a man who is just as kind, gentle, and loving as yours, but is also handsomer, sexier, and 100 times richer. Would you:
  A. Tell him to go away and leave you alone;
  or,
  B. Encourage him little by little until you are absolutely sure he's better (or worse) than the man you currently have?

12. You have hemorrhoids, which become inflamed and cause excruciating pain whenever you eat peanuts. You are in Georgia on business, and the person you are crazy about and trying desperately to impress invites you to dinner at his/her parents' home. The parents turn out to be peanut farmers and the entire dinner is made up of peanut-based dishes. Remember, you must do one of the following:
  A. Sacrifice your hemorrhoids for the sake of propriety and eat everything put in front of you;
  or,
  B. Patiently explain *exactly* what happens to your hemorrhoids as a result of eating peanuts.

13. Life has dealt you a losing hand. Your parents died when you were a child, your mate dumped you, you have a small penis or microscopic breasts, and a cancerous wart has begun to grow out of your forehead, which will be fatal within six months. You have no family, friends, or mate. To add insult to injury, the company you have worked for for 20 years has laid you off (along with 20,000 others) in order to "better serve the stockholders" and give the CEO a $100 million bonus. Would you rather:
  A. Commit suicide alone in your room;
  or,
  B. Walk into a board meeting with an AK-47 and take the CEO and some of those stockholders with you?

How You Stack Up

11. You tell the rich, handsome, sexy new man to leave you alone: 67%

    ... *or* you keep it going to see if he's better than your current beau: 33%.

12. You eat all the peanuts in front of you: 35%

    ... *or* begin a dinner table discussion of your hemorrhoids: 65%.

13. You commit suicide alone in your room: 14%

    ... *or* murder the entire board of directors with an assault rifle: 86%.

(SMITH AND DOE wish to note the shocking popularity of this option.)

14. Starfuckers Bonus Question: For years you have told all your friends you can't stand Barbra Streisand. You've never met her or even seen her in person but you know she's a shrill, homely witch. One day, out of the blue, you get a call: your Visa card number was selected in a raffle and you won a private dinner with Barbra: Would you:

A. Claim the prize, dine with Barbra, and bask in the glory of it;

or;

B. Write on the prize notification: "Fuck you, you witch. I wouldn't have dinner with you if I were out on the sidewalk dying of malnutrition"?

15. Remember poor little Baby Jessica, trapped in the bottom of that well as the world watched with white knuckles, praying for her safe return? Let's go back in time to when she was in that well. Would you:

A. Let things happen exactly as they did, with Baby Jessica getting saved;

or;

B. Have all of your debts mysteriously disappear from the memory banks of computers nationwide, but poor Baby Jessica never gets saved?

16. You have a plush job with a great salary and perks at the United Nations, but you've been reassigned to a committee that must go to a war-torn country where people are getting brutally massacred and you are literally risking your life. Would you:

A. Help initiate, negotiate, and sign a peace treaty, which ensures that no more innocent people get killed in this way again;

or;

B. Stay at home, instantly be gifted with fluency in two additional languages of your choice, leading to an even better job with more underlings?

How You Stack Up

14. You go to dinner with Barbra Streisand: 48%

... *or* reveal your true feelings and tell her to fuck off and die: 52%.

15. You allow Baby Jessica to be saved: 80%

... *or* erase your financial debts and let her die in the well: 20%.

16. You create a peace treaty, stopping a horrible war: 55%

... *or* get a promotion and whopping pay increase: 45%.

17. Remember that brave U.S. Air Force pilot who got shot down and spent 10 days hiding in the mud to avoid capture and was eventually rescued? Well, would you:

A. Let it happen exactly as it did;

or,

B. Be given the deed to your favorite house in the world (with no mortgage), but the brave airman gets hit by the blades on the chopper during the rescue and gets cut in half?

How You Stack Up

17. You let the air pilot escape in one piece: 50%

...*or* get your dream house while the pilot gets chopped in two: 50%.

Food

We all love it. Some of us each too much, some too little. But rarely do we eat things that are hideous in both concept and practice, unless of course we are offered outrageous sums of money by people we have never met . . .

1. **$5,000:** Empty a garbage pail, lift it up, and chug the liquid contents at the bottom.

2. **$10,000:** Dig through a garbage pail in a public place and eat all of the remaining food contents.

3. **$20,000:** Chug an entire bottle of Tabasco and wait ten minutes before drinking anything else (if you vomit, you must chug another bottle until you have successfully chugged and retained the contents).

4. **$250,000:** Have someone's spit from a spittoon (the result of tobacco dipping) inserted via an enema into your own butt. Then release the contents of your butt into a glass. Chug that and you've got the $250,000.

5. **$500,000:** Same as above, except it's Dennis Rodman's dip spit and Al Sharpton's butt juice that you have to chug.

6. **$1,000,000:** Same as above, except it's O. J's spit and Sammy Davis Jr.'s corpse's butt.

How You Stack Up

1. $5,000: Chug the garbage juice: 0%.

2. 10,000: Eat the garbage food: 0%.

3. $20,000: Chug a bottle of Tabasco: 13%.

4. $250,000: Chug the tobacco-spit enema: 0%.

5. $500,000: Chug the enema of Dennis Rodman's dip spit and Al Sharpton's butt juice (plus lots more $): 4%.

6. $1,000,000: . . . except it's O. J.'s spit and Sammy Davis Jr.'s corpse's butt: 14%. (Amazing what 10% more will do for an extra half-mil.)

7. 50,000: Bite the head off of a disease-free bat, chew, and
swallow it.

8. $500,000: Put the bat inside your butt while it is alive
and squeeze. Once the bat is dead from exhaustion and/or
suffocation, expel it from your butt, then bite its head off,
chew, and swallow it.

9. $2,500,000: With her consent, put the bat in your
mother's butt, wait until it's dead, then bite its head off,
chew, and swallow it. Wash it down with some blood from
the spewing torso of the bat.

10. $10,000,000: With his consent, put the bat in your fa-
ther's butt and give him a hand job until the bat is dead.
Then bite its head off, chew, and swallow it.

☺ ☺ ☺

11. $100,000: Release a long, hard piece of shit into the
toilet from your own butt. Pick up the log, put some salt on
it, and chow the whole thing. You may vomit, but you must
first chew and swallow the shit.

12. $500,000: Take only one bite of the shit, but swish it
around so that it gets stuck in your teeth, then swallow what
remains. You may not brush your teeth or eat or drink anything for the next twelve hours.

How You Stack Up

7. **$50,000:** Eat the bat head: 0%

8. **$500,000:** Cram the bat in your butt: 2%.

9. **$2,500,000:** Cram the bat in your mother's butt: 15%.

10. **$10,000,000:** Cram the bat in your father's butt, plus a handjob: 0%.

11. **$100,000:** Chow a log of your own shit: 13%.

12. **$500,000:** Swish it around in your mouth: 25%.

If Nobody Ever Knew, *Would You...*

This is one of our absolute favorites. It's simply a question of coming face to face with your own personal morality. They say an ideal society is based on the golden rule, "Do unto others as you would have them do unto you." But if, for one magical day, you could do anything you want to others and have nothing at all done to you, how would you really behave? Look into your darkest self and tell us the truth about what you would do...

1. **MEN:** Have wild sex with your teenage baby-sitter (or any other teenage girl)?

2. **WOMEN:** Have wild sex with your local high school's football or basketball star?

3. **WOMEN ONLY:** Have the man in your life kidnapped, surgically operated on to enlarge (or reduce) his penis and returned to you in perfect health? (Please state for the record, enlargement or reduction?)

4. **MEN ONLY:** Literally wring the neck of your mother-in-law or father-in-law, or, if you aren't married, anyone else in your mate's family?

5. Clean out and pocket the contents of a cash drawer from your local bank?

6. The entire safe? (What the hell, it's insured.)

7. Spike your IRS auditor's coffee with LSD (possibly causing him or her to jump off a building)?

8. Personally beat to a bruised and bloody pulp the preteenage neighborhood bully who has been picking on a child you know?

9. Put a thumbtack on your boss's seat and watch as he or she sits down?

How You Stack Up

1. 93% of men would have wild sex with a teenage baby-sitter.

2. 33% of women would have wild sex with a local high school football or basketball star.

3. 67% of women would welcome an operation on their mate's penis.

4. 46% of men would wring their in-law's neck.

5. 71% would rob a cash drawer.

6. 76% would rob the entire safe.

7. 70% would spike their auditor's drink with LSD.

8. 65% would beat a child bully to a bloody pulp.

9. 47% would put a thumbtack on their boss's seat.

10. Change that thumbtack to a rusty old nail and laugh as your boss runs out screaming for a tetanus shot?

11. Personally activate a remote-controlled poo-poo cushion you have planted on the Dalai Lama? (Before you jump at this opportunity, consider the negative spiritual effect it will have on his followers.)

12. Feed a steak filled with cut glass to any dog in your neighborhood?

13. Shoot in the head with a .57 Magnum the next person who says, "Been there; done that"?

14. Make sure your ex-wife or girlfriend NEVER has sex with a man who is blessed with a larger penis than yours?

15. Make sure your current husband or boyfriend never so much as glances at a younger-looking pair of breasts than yours?

16. Watch television for three days straight, breaking only for pizza, Chinese food, or sex with someone other than your mate?

17. Or just have lots of sex with someone other than your mate?

18. Draw a bull's-eye on top of the head of your least favorite bald person; then invite a class of troubled adolescents to see who can hit the bull's-eye with a palm-sized rock from a tenth-story window?

19. Urinate on someone's clean carpet?

20. Defecate on the driver's seat of your neighbor's car?

21. Plant a satchel of heroine in your landlord's room when he or she is asleep, then call the police, give them his or her address, and tell them a drug ring is operating out of the room.

22. Draw a cock and balls on your boss's forehead; then convince everyone at the office not to tell him it's there.

How You Stack Up

10. 36% would have their boss sit on a rusty old nail.

11. 53% would plant a poo-poo cushion on the Dalai Lama.

12. 12% would feed an annoying dog glass-filled steak.

13. 37% would shoot a vacuous person in the head.

14. 64% of men would guarantee that no ex will ever have sex with a guy with a bigger penis.

15. 60% of women would guarantee their man never so much as *glances* at a younger pair of breasts.

16. 73% would cheat on their mate while watching TV and chowing junk food.

17. 76% would cheat on their mate without the frills.

18. 41% would cause a rock to bust a bald enemy's head.

19. 59% would urinate on someone's clean carpet (dog envy?).

20. 40% would shit on the neighbor's car seat.

21. 53% would frame their landlord for drug possession.

22. 59% would tattoo a cock and balls on their boss's head.

23. Have the ability to detonate any vehicle via remote control that has a bumper sticker that annoys you?

24. MEN ONLY: When you glance seductively at the long-haired beauty in the car to your right and then make direct eye contact and realize it is a man, cause the man to go into immediate convulsions and have diarrhea in his pants, forcing him to pull over?

How You Stack Up

23. 75% would detonate the annoying vehicle.

24. 76% would force a stranger to convulse and have diarrhea while seated in his car.

Chapter Eleven

This category is the absolute litmus test of a true humanitarian. It has nothing to do with money. This is about your relationship to your fellowman, how you view the world you live in, where you feel you belong in the human food chain. If you're a lover of mankind, you'll find out here. If you're a miserable misanthrope, that too will become evident. In this category we give you the ultimate opportunity to prove yourself either a saint or a . . .

Selfish, Selfish Bastard!

1. In order to solve the world's hunger problems, would you bite, chew, and swallow the head of a live chicken?

2. MALES AND FEMALES: If you were guaranteed to live to a healthy 120 years of age with the body of a 30 year old, would you become a secret espionage agent, giving your country's secrets to Saddam Hussein?

3. If you are female, would you allow your vagina to be closed up forever in order to keep the looks of a 25 year old for the next 500 years?

4. What if you could live forever, but in order to do so your parents would have to die painfully at age 55?

5. Would you become the movie star of your choice if it meant losing the memory of everything about your present life?

6. What if you could become extremely rich and famous, but you would have no control over your bowels and be forced to wear Depends for the rest of your life?

How You Stack Up

1. Eat a live chicken head and cure world hunger: 55%.

2. Betray your country and live a long life: 34%.

3. Sew up your vagina but get lasting beauty: 50%.

4. Live forever but your parents croak early: 23%.

5. Lose your memory but become a movie star: 25%.

6. Win wealth and fame but lose bowel control: 34%.

7. What if you could become extremely rich and famous, but everyone you know would have to lose control of their bowels for the rest of their lives?

8. You have a net worth of $100,000. You can save every dying patient in every hospital in the world if you anonymously write a check for $98,000. Would you pay it?

9. You have saved up your whole life to buy your dream home. Once you've moved in, we offer you the following: give us your house and walk away with nothing, or keep the house but one of your closest friends will be tortured to death within the next three months.

10. You have a net worth of $50,000. If you anonymously write a $35,000 check, someone will discover a cure for Alzheimers. Would you write the check, assuming neither you nor anyone in your family will ever get Alzheimers?

11. You have a net worth of $50,000,000 and live a wonderful life on the beach with your wife and three kids. The entire world is going to be destroyed by a meteor in 50 years unless you all immediately swallow a poison drink and painlessly kill yourselves. Would you kill yourself and your family to save the earth or would you sacrifice the earth for another 50 years for your family?

12. What if you had the choice to let 100,000,000 random people on the earth die or only one of your family members (you must choose which one)?

How You Stack Up

7. Be rich and famous and let others shit their pants: 74%.

8. Give all you own to save dying patients: 43%.

9. You get your dream house but your friend gets tortured: 24%.

10. Give half your net worth to cure Alzheimers: 22%.

11. Sacrifice the earth now and gain 50 more years for your family: 64%.

12. Kill 100,000,000 strangers but save one member of your family: 55%.

Man's Best Friend

There's nothing cuter or more unconditionally loving than animals. You can do anything to them and they will always forgive you. Why? Partly because you love them back, but mainly because you provide shelter and friendship and buy them food and medical attention. Who (your own children excluded) wouldn't love you for that? But you must also bear in mind that animals are not human, they are easily acquired and cared for and plenty of Kevorkians are available when your pet starts to get lame and expensive. Therefore, thinking first and foremost of making a ton of money, consider these questions seriously . . .

1. $150,000: Your dog or cat will die in its sleep tonight.

2. $300,000: Your dog or cat will die painfully tonight.

3. $1,000,000: You must throw your dog or cat to its death off of a 20th-story balcony.

4. $1,500,000: You must be standing at the bottom of the building and watch as your dog or cat hits the pavement.

☺ ☺ ☺

5. $500,000: You must have oral sex with your dog until the dog has an orgasm.

6. $750,000: Same as above, except you must swallow.

7. $250,000: You must strangle your dog or cat to death with your bare hands.

Smith
and
Doe

90

How You Stack Up

1. Take the money and your pet dies peacefully tonight: 58%.

2. Take the money and your pet dies painfully tonight: 40%.

3. Take the money and throw your pet off the 20th-floor balcony: 29%.

4. Take the money and watch your pet explode when it hits the ground: 38%.

5. Take the money and blow your dog: 14%.

6. Take the money and swallow your dog's sperm: 10%.

7. Take the money and strangle your pet: 22%.

8. $500,000: You must strangle your dog or cat to death with your bare hands while you hold him/her inches away from your face, eye-to-eye.

9. $1,000,000: Put your dog/cat in the oven and watch as it slowly cooks to death.

10. $1,500,000: Put your dog/cat in the microwave, turn it on full, and wait for the explosion.

11. $250: Pick up your dog/cat's shit with your bare hands.

12. $500: Same as above, but you must squeeze it as hard as you can.

13. $5,000: Same as above, but you must wipe a generous helping of it on your nose and leave it there for one hour.

14. $10,000: Same as above, but you must spend the hour having dinner in a crowded restaurant.

15. $50,000: Same as above, but you must then complain to the waiter that your food tastes like dog/cat shit.

16. $100,000: Put a puppy or kitten into a trash compactor.

17. $500,000: Put a litter of puppies or kittens into a trash compactor.

How You Stack Up

8. Take the money and strangle your pet eye-to-eye: 18%.

9. Take the money and cook the pet: 9%.

10. Take the money and microwave the pet: 18%.

11. Take the money and pick up pet shit bare-handed: 65%.

12. Take the money and squeeze pet shit bare-handed: 66%.

13. Take the money and wear pet shit on your nose: 50%.

14. Take the money and wear pet shit to dinner at a restaurant: 42%.

15. Take the money, wear pet shit, and complain about the taste of your food: 54%.

16. Take the money and crush kitties or puppies in a trash compacter: 16%.

17. Take the money and compact a whole litter: 20%.

18. 10,000,000: Put a litter of puppies or kittens into a trash compactor, then send a photo of you with their squashed little bodies to your local newspaper.

How You Stack Up
18. Take the money, crush the kitties or puppies in the trash compactor; then brag about it in your local newspaper: 26%.

In the days of the Cold War, when the two superpowers had their mis-siles aimed at each other like a gunfight at the OK Corral, one man on each side had the final decision to make. One man: the president of the United States or the leader of the Soviet Union, had his finger on the red button. Now we place that same awesome power at your disposal, but no one on earth will know it but you. You're Kennedy. You're Khrushchev. You're Clinton. You're Hussein. You're the most powerful individual on earth and all you have to do is press that ...

All-Powerful Red Button

1. There is a red button in front of you. If you push it, **$250 million** will be deposited, tax free, into your personal account ... oh, and South Africa will plunge into the sea, killing millions of innocent people. Remember, nobody will find out it was you.

2. **$10,000,000:** Push the red button in front of you and 100 random people under age 30 from around the world will die of natural causes. You are guaranteed not to know any of the people or ever hear about their deaths.

3. **$1,000,000,000:** That's $1 billion. If you push the red button in front of you, the United States will sink into the ocean in 60 days. You can warn as many people as you want, assuming any of them will believe you. You will live in the country of your choice with your family, all of the friends that would listen to you, and your new-found $1,000,000,000.

4. **$50,000:** There is a red button in front of you. If you push it, one of your close friends will lose two of his toes in a random acci-dent. Life will go on as usual without the two toes, and, of course, your friend will have no idea you had anything to do with it.

5. **$1,500,000:** If you push the red button in front of you; one of your coworkers (you don't get to choose) will begin to have a se-vere, embarrassing twitch in the left side of his/her face for the rest of their life. People will stare at this person for the rest of their life and make fun of him/her.

96 How You Stack Up

1. Take the $250 million and lose South Africa: 58%.

2. Take the $10 million and young people die: 55%.

3. Take the billion and family and say good-bye to the U.S.A.: 38%.

4. Take the 50 grand but chop off friend's toes: 16%.

5. Take a half-million but your coworker twitches: 35%.

6. $500,000 **WOMEN ONLY:** If you push the red button in front of you, every man in the world who has ever cheated on his wife will die of a heart attack. WARNING: You risk depleting the world population to dangerous levels, as well as the murder of your own spouse, father, and loved ones.

7. $100 **MEN ONLY:** If you push the button in front of you, you will be able to sexually attain any female in the world you want. The catch is that you will never have another relationship that lasts more than three days and you will never have children.

8. $0: Same as above, except you may have children out of wedlock.

9. There's a red button in front of you. If you push it, you will become a billionaire, president of the United States, and drop-dead gorgeous. But every time you pee, it will feel like a scalding hot iron is being forced into your urinary tract.

How You Stack Up

6. **WOMEN:** Take a half-mil and men who cheat die: 65%.

7. **MEN:** Take 100 bucks, have great sex, but no kids: 24%.

8. **MEN:** Get no money, but have great sex, and no wife: 30%.

9. Take a billion, become a VIP with hot pee: 26%.

Priorities

What is your actual net worth, without inflating the equity in your home, the value of that Impressionist painting your parents left you, or that overpriced luxury car you finally paid off? Is it $20,000? $75,000? $500,000? $1,000,000 or more? Whatever it is, keep it; it's yours. SMITH AND DOE have deposited $250,000 in a special bank account, all of which you must spend in this next category. (This means you must pick 5 of the 20 items, based on their importance to you.) We invite you to go on a wild shopping spree at our expense.

FROM YOUR $250,000 SMITH AND DOE BANK ACCOUNT, WHICH OF THESE ITEMS WILL YOU PURCHASE?

(NOTE: you must spend the $250,000, not a penny more or less.)

Item	Cost
1. Stop an impending earthquake in Albania that will kill millions.	$50,000
2. Stop impending baldness and guarantee that you will never lose your hair.	$50,000
3. Guarantee that you will be 100% healthy and fertile, but will never have to deal with your period again.	$50,000

Smith *and* Doe

100

4. Guarantee there are no civilian casualties in the next middleeast war. $50,000

5. Go back and undo the Holocaust, bringing everyone who died back to life. $50,000

6. Go back in time and relive the best sexual experience you've ever had? $50,000

7. Reprogram the world's computers so that no one is ever evicted from their home and thrown out on the street. $50,000

8. Reprogram the bank's computers so that your ATM card never actually takes the money out of your account. $50,000

9. Guarantee that there is never another war on earth for the rest of time. $50,000

10. Guarantee that you can sexually attain anyone you want for the rest of your life. $50,000

11. Ensure that AIDS is cured within the next three years. $50,000

12. Ensure that every light you drive through will be green for the rest of your life. $50,000

13. Make sure that the United States never falls victim to another terrorist act. $50,000

14. Make sure that you get promoted every year with a big raise for the rest of your life. $50,000

15. Provide that no one will ever be murdered for the rest of eternity (beginning with the day you die)? $50,000

16. Provide that every elevator you approach will have its doors open and no one else will ever ride with you? $50,000

17. Give $10,000,000 anonymously to your favorite hospital. $50,000

18. Give $10,000,000 to your favorite hospital and have a wing named after you. $50,000

19. Have a deep realization that God is within you and you are one with the universe. $50,000

20. Have everyone else have a deep realization that God is within *you*, and therefore you are smarter and better looking than they are. $50,000

Smith
and
Doe

How You Stack Up

1. 7% stopped the earthquake in Albania.

2. 3% stopped their own baldness.

3. 3% stopped having periods.

4. 3% saved lives in the next middleeast war.

5. 9% brought everyone back from the Holocaust.

6. 5% relieved their best sexual experience.

7. 4% put an end to homelessness.

8. 9% took endless money from ATM's.

9. 12% guaranteed no more war on earth.

10. 11% sexually attained anyone they wanted.

11. 11% cured AIDS in three years.

12. 2% insured green traffic lights for life.

13. 1% stopped terrorism in the U.S.A.

14. 3% got promotions and pay bumps every year.

15. 6% stopped murder for eternity.

16. 1% took private elevators.

17. 1% gave anonymous millions to a hospital.

18. 3% took credit for giving millions to hospital.

19. 2% realized God is within themselves.

20. 4% had others see that God is within them and that they are smarter and more beautiful than anyone else.

You are in the majority if you:

1. Brought everyone back from the Holocaust

2. Took endless money from ATM's

3. Guaranteed no more war on earth

4. Sexually attained anyone you wanted, and

5. Cured AIDS in 3 years.

Incest on Sale

You might have thought this category too touchy a subject, even for us. Well, you're wrong. Remember Scrooge McDuck? How you loved to see him diving into huge pools of money and picture yourself doing the same? Remember that Lotto ticket you buy every week that you know in your heart you don't have a prayer to win? Well, here's your chance for the score of a lifetime. Imagine that mansion in Aspen, the parties you'll throw for Jack Nicholson, Sharon Stone, and John Travolta. Imagine the skis strapped to the top of your stretch Mercedes limo, waving good-bye to the elk in your backyard, looking at the rest of the world through expensively tinted windows.

And what do you have to do for it?

1. $10,000,000. **(WOMEN):** You will be required to perform oral sex on your father until orgasm. You can discuss the proposal with him, work on it together, and share the money if you wish. **(MEN):** You will be required to perform oral sex on your mother until orgasm. Same rules. (NOTE: A licensed gynecologist must be present to verify that your mother is not faking her orgasm.)

2. $7,500,000. Same as above, except involving brothers and sisters.

3. $10,000. **(MEN):** In a dark movie theater, slip your hand under your sister's clothing and fondle her bare breast. (You may explain how much you are getting paid while you are doing it.)

4. $25,000: Same as above, except fondle her genitals.

5. $15,000. **(WOMEN):** Same as above, but fondle your brother's penis.

6. $25,000: Same as above, but fondle his penis until erect.

106 How You Stack Up

1. 2% of women would blow Daddy; 9% of men would bring Mommy to orgasm.

2. 0% of women would blow brother; 2% of men would bring sister to orgasm.

3. 50% would feel up sister.

4. 26% would fondle sister's genitals.

5. 3% would fondle brother's penis.

6. 6% would fondle brother's penis to erection.

7. $50,000. (**MEN AND WOMEN**): Same as above, but bring your sibling to climax.

☺ ☺ ☺

8. $10,000: French kiss your mother or father in public.

9. $20,000: Same as above, ***without*** explaining why you did it.

☺ ☺ ☺

10. $250,000: Impregnate or be impregnated by a first cousin.

11. $500,000: Keep the baby, regardless of how many ears or toes it has.

☺ ☺ ☺

12. $250,000: Stand in front of your parents' bed with the lights on and watch them have sex until orgasm.

13. $400,000: Stand in front of your parents' bed with the lights on and watch your mother give your father a blow job.

14. $1,000,000: Stand in front of your parents' bed with the lights on and watch your father have anal sex with your mother. **$250,000** bonus if you attempt to masturbate while this is taking place.

☺ ☺ ☺

15. $200,000: Allow your mother or father to watch you have sex with your mate with the lights on.

16. $300,000: Allow both your mother and father to watch you give a blow job to your mate with the lights on.

Smith
and
Doe

How You Stack Up

7. 27% would bring sibling to climax.

8. 9% would french kiss parent in public.

9. 9% would french kiss without explanation.

10. 42% would impregnate (or be impregnated by) first cousin.

11. 16% would keep possibly deformed cousin baby.

12. 42% would watch parents copulate.

13. 36% would watch parents have oral sex.

14. 40% would watch parents have anal sex.

15. 41% would allow parent to watch them have sex.

16. 2% would allow parents to watch them oral sex with mate.

17. $500,000: Allow both your mother and father to have sex in the same room with you while you have sex with your mate with the lights on.

☺ ☺ ☺

18. $10,000: Clean the skid marks from a hamperful of your mother or father's dirty underwear using a toothbrush and bar of soap.

19. $100,000: Same as above, except using only your tongue.

Enough Money To Last You Forever

20. $5,000,000. **(MEN):** Chew on your mother's used tampon for 3 minutes.

21. $10,000,000. **(WOMEN):** Drink from your father's used condom.

MEN:

22. $25,000: Suck on your mother's nipple for 5 minutes, with her full knowledge that you are getting paid and with her full compliance.

23. $250,000: Suck on your mother's nipple for 5 minutes, and every minute stop and for 15 seconds stare her in the eye and talk dirty to her, then continue sucking. SMITH AND DOE must choose what you will say, so trust us, it will be very dirty.

24. $1,000,000: Suck on your mother's nipple for 5 minutes, and for the last 2 minutes begin fingering her.

Smith *and* Doe

110 **How You Stack Up**

17. 31% would have orgy with parents.

18. 64% would clean parents' skid marks.

19. 11% would clean parent's skid marks by tongue.

20. 50% would chew on Mommy's used tampon.

21. 3% would drink from Daddy's used condom.

22. 29% would suck on Mommy's nipples.

23. 14% would suck nipples and talk dirty.

24. 14% would suck nipples and finger Mommy.

MEN:

25. $250,000: Whip out your penis in front of your mother and, in dead seriousness, tell her you want her to "kiss it." You may never tell her you got paid, and if she elects to kiss it (or more, if you're lucky), you must let her have her way. If you ever tell her the truth about why you did it, you will never again be able to have an orgasm as long as you live.

26. $1,500,000: Whip out your penis in front of your mother, tell her you want her to watch as you "work the shaft," begin to masturbate, and if she's still in the room at this point, ask her to lick the underside of your balls to help you achieve orgasm. You may never tell her you got paid, and same rules regarding the orgasm apply to this question.

WOMEN:

27. $25,000: Tell your father you want to ask him a personal question. Sit him down and, in all seriousness, tell him that you want him to shave your vagina for you because you are not comfortable doing it yourself. You get paid regardless of whether or not he complies, as long as you never confess to getting paid.

28. $50,000: Tell your father that as part of a science project you want to shave his balls. If you don't persuade him to let you, you don't get paid.

29. $500,000: Same as above, except you must grab the shaft and begin jerking it until he leaps away in disgust.

30. $1,000,000: Same as above, except you must try to suck it.

31. $1,250,000: Same as above, except you must beg him to let you continue once he jumps away in horror.

How You Stack Up

25. 1% would tell Mom to kiss their penis.

26. 2% would tell Mom to "work the shaft."

27. 5% would ask Dad to shave their vagina.

28. 2% would ask to shave Dad's balls.

29. 0% would work Dad's shaft.

30. 0% would work Dad's shaft and suck.

31. 0% would force Dad to take it.

MEN AND WOMEN:

32. $25,000: At the next family wedding, approach your best-looking first cousin and tell him/her that you have always wanted to "make love to them" and would they like to go upstairs for a little "family values"? Whether or not they agree, you can never tell them why you asked.

33. $250,000: During a family wedding, get up to make a toast and tell the family that you have mixed feelings about the wedding because you are secretly in love with the person getting married (a close family member). When everyone laughs, you must dead seriously explain, as you begin to cry, how painful it is for you; then you must run away and hide for three days.

34. $500,000: Same as above, except as you run away you must yell that the person getting married has an airborne virus that causes genital herpes.

Smith
and
Doe

114 **How You Stack Up**

32. 37% would proposition first cousin at family function.

33. 12% would disgrace themselves at family wedding.

34. 15% would fully mortify themselves with family.

A Crazed Madman Has a Gun!

Imagine a crazed lunatic. Now imagine the same crazed lunatic holding a loaded gun to your head with one bullet left—and right now, it's got your name on it. You can either take the bullet, or . . .

1. Direct it at your 70-year-old mother or your 72-year-old father. They plead with you; they have lived a full life and either would seemingly prefer taking the bullet. What will it be—you or one of them?

2. The madman gives you a choice. You can either take a bullet to the head, or he will cut off your genitals, amputate your right arm, and stick a hot, burning stick into your right eye. He will then leave you for dead; and in the unlikely event that you are found and saved, you will spend the rest of your life disfigured. Shoot or don't shoot?

3. The madman gives you another choice. You can either take a bullet to the chest (a wound from which you might survive), or he will rape you (doesn't matter if you are a man or a woman). Once the rape is completed, he will then force you to bite off, chew, and swallow 3 of your own fingers. Once you have chewed and swallowed the limbs, you are free to go. Which do you choose?

4. You are standing on a beach by the foul, rotting corpse of a sea lion. The madman is pointing the gun at your head. He tells you that you can either painlessly take a bullet to the head and die right now; or, within a 24-hour period you must eat the entire corpse of the sea lion, including the skin but excluding the bones, and you are permitted to vomit a maximum of 3 times during the meal. Once you have finished this feast, you are free to go. Do you eat or die?

116 **How You Stack Up**

1. You die: 41%
   ... or one of your parents dies: 59%.

2. Take a bullet in the head: 80%
   ... or lose your genitals: 20%.

3. Take a bullet in your chest: 79%
   ... or eat your own fingers: 21%.

4. Take a bullet in your head: 38%
   ... or eat stinky dead sea lion: 62%.

5. The madman didn't sleep very well last night and is in a foul mood. He tells you that he is going to kill you unless you slice both of your wrists so that you are bleeding heavily and then swim out into the nearby shark-infested waters, where you must tread water for 10 minutes. If you survive, you may bandage up your wrists and leave. If you get eaten by the sharks, well, you get eaten by the sharks. Die, or take your chances with the sharks?

6. The madman has taken you to the top of a 30-story building. You are standing on the ledge overlooking a seemingly endless fall to the concrete below. The madman, pointing a gun at you, explains to you that if you jump, you will die instantly when you hit the pavement. If you don't jump, he is going to shoot you in the gut, then the genitals, and let you bleed to death up here. Of course, there is a slim chance of rescue, but a very slim one. (The madman, if you haven't already learned, is a crack shot and would never miss, so trying to jump him would result in instant death.) Do you jump or take the bullets?

7. The madman is in a worse mood than before. He tells you that he is going to have a horrible bout of diarrhea at any given moment. He also feels that he wants to shoot you in the head. But if you put your mouth on his butt and drink every drop of diarrhea, and top it off with a wonderful blow job at the end of which you swallow, he will let you go. NOTE: If any diarrhea or sperm escapes your mouth, you will be killed. Suck butt or take the bullet?

8. Now the madman is horny. He says that if you let him "fist" you (which means putting his actual hand inside your butt and pushing up until his hand, up to the midwrist, is inserted in your anus), he will let you go. If not, he'll cut off a breast if you're a woman or a testicle if you're a man and leave you to die. You may survive, but who knows? Anyone in their right mind would go for the fist over the bullet. Would you?

How You Stack Up

5. Die painfully: 40%

   ... or take your chances with sharks: 60%.

6. Get shot in gut and genitals: 53%

   ... or jump 30 stories: 47%.

7. Suck diarrhea from madman's butt: 19%

   ... or take the bullet: 81%.

8. Take the fist: 68%

   ... or take the bullet: 32%.

9. The madman has just eaten an entire bottle of Viagra. He
says that he wants to have unprotected anal sex all night
long, and you must pretend that you are loving every minute
of it or you will be killed. If you make a sound that indicates
you aren't having the best time you've ever had, you will be
killed. If you cause him to stop for any reason, you will be
killed. And he hasn't had an AIDS test in years. Dangerous
anal sex, or a bullet in the head. What will it be?

10. The madman takes you to the Brooklyn Bridge in the
dead of night. Directly below, a ship carrying wooden spikes
is anchored. The spikes are pointing up and there are thou-
sands of them. The madman hands you a bungie cord that is
three-quarter's of the way torn in the middle. You can either
tie the bungee cord and jump straight at the spikes (if the
rope doesn't rip and you bounce back up, you may leave un-
harmed) or you can jump straight into the water and die instantly. Your choice.

11. The madman is thirsty. He explains that he is either
going to kill you, or he will allow you to live if you let him
drink blood directly from your slit wrist for 3 minutes. You
may faint and die, or you may live, depending on how much
he drinks. If you are alive when he is done drinking, you
may go. If you elect not to allow him to drink, he will shoot
you in the head. He drinks or you die—a no-brainer, right?

12. The madman is hungry. He explains that he is either
going to kill you, or he will allow you to live if you let him
amputate and eat your right foot. He will amputate it with
no anesthesia, and cauterize the wound with a hot poker
from the fireplace. But you will survive, and he won't be
hungry anymore. The last catch is that you must sit and
watch him eat your foot until he is done, then you may go.
(He'll also provide a comfortable pair of crutches.) What
will it be?

How You Stack Up

9. Dangerous anal sex for hours: 33%
 . . . or bullet in your head: 67%.

10. Bungee jump onto spikes: 87%
 . . . or die instantly: 13%.

11. Madman drinks your blood: 87%
 . . . or he shoots you in the head: 13%.

12. Madman kills you: 27%
 . . . or he eats your foot: 73%.

Chapter Seventeen

The Smith and Doe Low-Rent Celebrity Auction

Once again, SMITH AND DOE are bankrolling a special shopping spree just for you. We've got some seriously hot collector's items here, and we mean to test your instinctive sense of investment. We want you to buy only those items that you believe will increase most in value in 10 years. Let's see how much you can make. We're putting $50,000 cash in your hand with the one condition that you spend every last cent of it. (At the end of the auction, having consulted our inside source at Christie's Auction House, we reveal the actual, 10-year projected value of each item.)

ITEM	YOUR WINNING BID
1. The original Monica Lewinsky–Linda Tripp tapes.	$10,000
2. Assuming it exists, actual videotape of Monica blowing the prez.	$20,000
3. The panties Princess Diana wore on her last night with Dodi.	$10,000
4. Dodi's underwear, preserved from the moment of impact.	$250
5. An original, unretouched photo of Abraham Lincoln romping with a hairless Filipino boy.	$4,000
6. Hitler's foreskin (with certificate of authenticity signed by Kurt Waldheim).	$25,000
7. 8 ounces of collagen taken from Rock Hudson's lips.	$1,500
8. John Goodman's personal toilet seat	$3,500
9. Saddam Hussein's first Barbie doll (wounds inflicted by young Saddam himself).	$5,000

How You Stack Up

1. *Lewinsky-Tripp tapes:*
   CHOSEN BY 36%
   COST AT AUCTION TODAY: $10,000
   In ten years hardly anyone will remember the Big Lewinsky.
   VALUE TEN YEARS FROM NOW: $3,000
   LOSS: $7,000

2. *Presidential XXX video:*
   CHOSEN BY 98%
   COST AT AUCTION TODAY: $20,000
   Presidential blow-job videos will always be valuable, regardless of who the mouth belongs to.
   VALUE TEN YEARS FROM NOW: $40,000
   PROFIT: $20,000

3. *Diana's panties:*
   CHOSEN BY 70%
   COST AT AUCTION TODAY: $10,000
   A no-brainer.
   VALUE TEN YEARS FROM NOW: $10,000,000
   PROFIT: $9,990,000

4. *Dodi's panties:*
   CHOSEN BY 3%
   COST AT AUCTION TODAY: $250
   Not worth the silk it's shitted on.
   VALUE TEN YEARS FROM NOW: $10
   LOSS: $150

5. *Lincoln with naked boy photo:*
   CHOSEN BY 38%
   COST AT AUCTION TODAY: $4,000
   Trick question: a photo that old is worth the same as it will be ten years from now.
   VALUE TEN YEARS FROM NOW: $5,500
   PROFIT: $1,500

6. *Hitler's foreskin:*
   CHOSEN BY 11%
   COST AT AUCTION TODAY: $25,000
   Since Kurt Waldheim was not in Hitler's inner sanctum, his veracity is doubtful. A mere novelty item.
   VALUE TEN YEARS FROM NOW: $25
   LOSS: $24,975

7. *Rock's collagen:*
   CHOSEN BY 5%
   COST AT AUCTION TODAY: $1,500
   Movie collectors are rabid, pay to top price for anything.
   VALUE TEN YEARS FROM NOW: $10,000
   PROFIT: $8,500

8. *John Goodman's toilet seat:*
   CHOSEN BY 14%
   COST AT AUCTION TODAY: $3,500
   More flashy than Rock's collagen, but Goodman's not as big a star.
   VALUE TEN YEARS FROM NOW: $4,500
   PROFIT: $1,000

9. *Saddam's Barbie doll:*
   CHOSEN BY 40%
   COST AT AUCTION TODAY: $5,000
   Not on a par with Hitler's real foreskin, but precious all the same.
   VALUE TEN YEARS FROM NOW: $25,000
   PROFIT: $20,000

ITEM	YOUR WINNING BID
10. A single hair taken from Garth Brooks's butt.	$20,000
11. A single hair taken from Rosanne Barr's butt.	$5
12. A jar containing Mama Cass's last chunks.	$250
13. A personal tour of John Wayne and Liberace's secret homosexual hideaway, complete with sex toys and domination equipment.	$500
14. Madonna's child's first bronzed baby turds.	$2,500
15. Cindy Crawford's bicycle seat (hermetically sealed immediately following a 30-mile ride in 100-degree heat).	$3,500
16. One centiliter of biologically preserved semen donated by George Clooney.	$3,500
17. MYSTERY PRIZE: The unexamined contents of Pee Wee Herman's dresser drawers.	$5,000
18. S/M BUFFS: The Gimp's leather costume from *Pulp Fiction* (including red mouth ball).	$5,000
19. The preserved cancer sore that was removed from Ronald Reagan's nose.	$5,000
20. Hillary Clinton's actual diary.	$10,000

How You Stack Up

10. Garth's butt-hair:
CHOSEN BY 1%
COST AT AUCTION TODAY: $20,000
Even for Brooks fanatics, one dingleberry is a hard resell.
(Though those people are no strangers to dingleberries.)
VALUE TEN YEARS FROM NOW: $20
LOSS: $19,980

11. Rosanne's butt-hair:
CHOSEN BY 12%
COST AT AUCTION TODAY: $5
Different from Garth's in that it's a true conversation
piece—plus the dingleberry itself has greater heft.
VALUE TEN YEARS FROM NOW: $5,000
PROFIT: $4,995

12. Mama Cass vomit:
CHOSEN BY 2%
COST AT AUCTION TODAY: $250
Ugh!
VALUE TEN YEARS FROM NOW: $0
LOSS: $250

13. The homo tour:
CHOSEN BY 22%
COST AT AUCTION TODAY: $500
VALUE TEN YEARS FROM NOW:
Nothing left but pianos and guns.
LOSS: $500

14. Madonna's baby's turds:
CHOSEN BY 41%
COST AT AUCTION TODAY: $2,500
Basically worthless except for one critical element—
Madonna herself, who will buy them back from you.
VALUE TEN YEARS FROM NOW: $10,000
PROFIT: $7,500

15. Cindy's bicycle seat:
    CHOSEN BY 57%
    COST AT AUCTION TODAY: $3,500
    A smart purchase at any price: If hermetically sealed and
    never opened for the full 10 years . . .
    VALUE TEN YEARS FROM NOW: $50,000
    PROFIT: $46,500

16. Clooney's semen:
    CHOSEN BY 20%
    COST AT AUCTION TODAY: $3,500
    Considering the progress in fertilization techniques, this
    would have been worth millions if Clooney had not mar-
    keted more sperm than Ted Williams did baseball cards.
    VALUE TEN YEARS FROM NOW: $100,000
    PROFIT: $96,500

17. Pee Wee's sex toys:
    CHOSEN BY 15%
    COST AT AUCTION TODAY: $5,000
    Though Pee-Wee ain't what he used to be, celebrity wor-
    shippers will always pony up for toys like this.
    VALUE TEN YEARS FROM NOW: $7,500
    PROFIT: $2,500

18. "Pulp Fiction" Gimp's leather costume:
    CHOSEN BY 39%
    COST AT AUCTION TODAY: $5,000
    Not only major memorabilia, but suitable for personal
    use.
    VALUE TEN YEARS FROM NOW: $30,000
    PROFIT: $25,000

19. Reagan's cancer sore:
    CHOSEN BY 15%
    COST AT AUCTION TODAY: $5,000
    Recently classified "a weapon of mass destruction," this
    sore was made unavailable at auction time. (Reagan for-

got where he put it. Then he forgot what he was looking
for. Then he forgot he was trying to remember what he
was looking for.)
VALUE TEN YEARS FROM TODAY: N/A
PROFIT/LOSS:N/A

20. *Hillary's diary:*
CHOSEN BY 75%
COST AT AUCTION TODAY: $10,000
More than 50 diaries purporting to be the genuine article
are anticipated to surface over the next 10 years. (If you
had checked this particular item during a preauction in-
vestigation, you would know that, on p. 34 The First Lady
claims that Bill is a "faithful loving husband" therefore
proving this just another forgery.)
VALUE TEN YEARS FROM NOW: $0
LOSS: $10,000

It's like the SAT's except a little more graphic ... YOU MUST CHOOSE AN ANSWER, no if's, and's, or but's. Steel yourself for a grueling test of your preferences and try your hand at ...

Life Choices

Multiple Choice: *(You must choose either A, B, OR C).*

1.A. Kill a deer by bludgeoning it to death with a sledgehammer.
B. Jerk off a horse to orgasm.
C. Stick your arm up a cow's ass to the elbow (assuming the cow doesn't resist).

2.A. Jump into an ice-fishing hole.
B. Walk barefoot through an acre of dog diarrhea.
C. Stick your head in a bucket of hot tar.

3. *Pick one of these moments in which you will become afflicted with an uncontrollable blast of Montezuma's revenge:*
A. While being introduced to your boyfriend/girlfriend's parents.
B. While entering the crowded, coed steam bath at your local health club.
C. Walking past the three most attractive boys/girls at a nudist colony.

128 **How You Stack Up**

1.A. Brutally kill Bambi: 24%
   B. Jerk off a horse: 29%
   C. Stick your arm up a cow's ass: 47%.

2.A. Jump into an ice-fishing hole: 53%
   B. Walk through dog shit: 47%
   C. Stick your head in hot tar: 0%

3.A. Shit in front of your mate's parents: 41%
   B. Shit in the steam bath: 24%.
   C. Shit at the nudist colony: 35%.

4. *Signing your real name and address, would you:*
A. Write a threatening letter to Bill Clinton (thereby placing yourself on the FBI Watch List).
B. Write an erotically charged love letter to the most repulsive man or woman you work with.
C. Write to your parents confessing the truth about the most offensive sexual act you've ever engaged in.

5. *Using only the excuse of "temporary insanity":*
A. Smash your neighbor's brand new Mercedes with a sledgehammer.
B. Drive the wrong way on a one-way street in rush hour.
C. Using a realistic-looking toy gun, hold up a city bus driver.

6. *Admitting SMITH AND DOE paid you money to do it, would you:*
A. Pinch a uniformed policeman's ass.
B. Blow your nose and wipe it on your sleeve at a job interview.
C. Repeatedly jump up and down as hard as you can in an overcrowded elevator.

7.A. Have your anal glands squeezed by a competent veterinarian, causing immediate full release.
B. Lose a fingernail by closing a car door on it.
C. Have a benign tumor removed from your ear with a pair of pliers.

How You Stack Up

4.A. Write a hate letter to Bill Clinton: 11%.
 B. Write an erotic letter to repulsive person: 48%.
 C. Describe a sex act to your parents: 41%.

5.A. Smash your neighbor's Mercedes: 40%.
 B. Drive the wrong way on a one-way street: 40%.
 C. Hold up a city bus driver: 20%.

6.A. Pinch a policeman's ass: 21%.
 B. Blow your nose and wipe on sleeve: 26%.
 C. Jump up and down in overcrowded elevator: 53%.

7.A. Have anal glands squeezed: 48%.
 B. Crush fingernail in car door: 40%.
 C. Pull tumor from ear with pliers: 12%.

8.A. Get your foot run over by an 18-wheeler, shattering every bone in it.
B. Get your hand caught in a meat grinder.
C. Put your mouth on the red-hot exhaust pipe of a car for 30 seconds.

How You Stack Up

8.A. Get foot run over by 18-wheeler: 91%.

B. Get hand caught in meat grinder: 0%.

C. Put mouth on red hot exhaust pipe: 9%.

9.A. Have a roach crawl in your ear while you are sleeping, which attempts to burrow its way into your brain but is dead when you wake up and has caused no real damage.
B. Have a mouse crawl into your anus while you are asleep, which you discover only during your next visit to the bathroom.
C. Allow a small band of red ants to climb into your nostril and feast on your mucus while you sleep, only to awake you by the itching sensation caused by their chowing.

10. *Keeping in mind that you MUST choose one of these . . .*
A. Eat the four-week-old, rotting carcass of a small sheep.
B. Eat the 4-week-old, rotting carcass of a human train accident victim.
C. Eat the 4-week-old, rotting carcass of your neighbor's recently deceased cat.

11.A. Get shot by an intruder in the leg.
B. Get shot by an intruder in the arm.
C. Get shot by an intruder in the shoulder.

How You Stack Up

9.A. Roach crawl in ear: 56%.
  B. Mouse crawl in anus: 13%.
  C. Red ants in nostril: 31%.

10.A. Eat sheep carcass: 5%.
  B. Eat train victim carcass: 12%.
  C. Eat neighbor's cat carcass: 33%.

11.A. Get shot in leg: 32%.
  B. Get shot in arm: 48%.
  C. Get shot in shoulder: 20%.

12. *During a robbery of your home, you either. . . .*

A. Shoot the assailant in the stomach, disabling him until the police arrive.

B. Shoot the assailant in the kneecaps, disabling him until the police arrive.

C. Shoot the assailant in the head, killing him instantly.

How You Stack Up

12.A. Shoot assailant in stomach: 9%.

B. Shoot assailant in kneecaps: 54%.

C. Shoot assailant in head: 37%.

13.A. Have one incredible night of torrid sex.

B. Find **$500** on the sidewalk.

C. Have a free dinner at your favorite restaurant with your best friends.

☺ ☺ ☺

14. *Think of someone you genuinely hate (we all hate someone, especially when you really think about it). Keeping in mind you have no choice but to choose one of the answers, would you elect for this person to . . .*

A. Get hit by a bus, thus rendered paralyzed for life.

B. Fall off of a lawnmower and subsequently be disfigured for life but live.

C. Get in an accident that causes the full amputation of all sexual genitalia?

How You Stack Up

13.A. Incredible night of sex: 46%.

   B. Find **$500** on sidewalk: 41%.

   C. Free dinner at favorite restaurant: 13%.

14.A. Enemy hit by a bus: 5%.

   B. Enemy disfigured by lawnmover: 29%.

   C. Enemy's genitalia amputated: 66%.

No Price on Earth

In closing, there are very few things in this world that people would not do for money. But even SMITH AND DOE have to admit that for what follows, there is simply no price on earth...

Eat the 1-year-old carcass of a dead, immediate family member.

Barbecue your first-born child alive on a spit.

Amputate your own genitalia.

Put a spaghetti-thin, red-hot poker 3 inches into your penis for 2 full minutes.

Detach the brake lines from your mother's car.

Play Russian roulette with a gun that has 5 of 6 chambers loaded.

Attempt to jump over an 8-foot chasm bubbling with molten lava.

Lay face down on a pile of red-hot embers for 3 full minutes.

Chug a glass of sulfuric acid.

Stick your head in a trash compactor.

Lubricate a string of 100 firecrackers, push them up your butt one by one, leaving the last one hanging out, then light the fuse.

140 On Christmas Eve, hammer a nail deep enough into your forehead to hang your Christmas stocking on.

Perform a requested abortion on a woman who's 8 months pregnant.

Dice your own tongue with a razor blade and swallow the pieces.

Drop your pants and squirt a stream of diarrhea on the pope's shoes (while he's wearing them).

Walk around for a week with an actual severed penis hanging from your mouth.

And last, but not least . . .

Answer *any question* put to you in public by SMITH AND DOE 100% truthfully.

Interactive

Here's your chance to jump in the muck and wallow around with SMITH AND DOE. Fill in the blanks with your own personal choices for...

No Price on Earth

Eat the_____ of a recently deceased family member.

Barbecue _____ alive on the spit.

Amputate_____ with no anesthesia.

Put a _____ into your _____ for two full minutes.

Detach _____ from your mother's _____.

Play _____ with a

_____ .

Attempt to _____ over a

_____ .

Lay face down on _____ .

Chug a _____ .

Stick your _____ in a

_____ .

Lubricate _____ , push them into your

_____ one by one, then

_____ .

142   On Christmas Eve, _____ in your
_____ and hang your Christmas stocking on it.

Perform _____ on an unwilling
_____ .

Dice _____ with a razor blade and
_____ .

Drop your pants and _____ on
_____ shoes.

Walk around for a week with a _____
hanging from your _____ .

And last but not least . . .

Answer any question put to you in public by
_____ 100% truthfully.